THE FORTIES IN

THE FORTIES IN
VOGUE

CAROLYN HALL
FOREWORD BY
PETER USTINOV

OCTOPUS BOOKS

Designed by STEVE KIBBLE

First published in 1985 by
Octopus Books Limited
59 Grosvenor Street
London W1

Produced by Mandarin Publishers Limited
22a Westlands Road
Quarry Bay, Hong Kong

Printed in Hong Kong

Contents

6

Foreword

As life lengthens, it is more and more difficult to segregate the decades from each other, and to speak with the admirable lucidity of some critics about the marked changes which characterise each ten-year period in this century. Apart from which I am no Boswell. I am not even a diarist, although I do recognise the approach of old age, not because of any physical infirmity, thank goodness, but by the fact of recurrent waves of 'retro', in obedience to a nostalgia for periods I have experienced at first hand.

The mode of life in the first half of the Forties was, of course, dictated by war. There was no catering to male vanity in the drab uniformity of our clothes, and the women, under the heartily heroic aegis of the slogan 'make-do and mend', fared not much better. Waiters in restaurants took not only the bill, but ration-cards, and gas-masks were suspended from the backs of chairs in case of a sudden gas attack during dinner. At night, the taxis crept around the blackened streets with Fu-Manchu slits over their headlights, and as often as not the nostrils were assailed by the sickening smell of burning buildings, while the sky seemed to have a deep orange pulse.

It all seems curiously unreal today, and it seemed as curiously unreal the very moment it was over, when, with a sudden relaxation of tension, the people voted in a Labour government, an action absolutely in accordance with the mood of the moment, but one which appeared, especially to Americans, an act of treachery towards Churchill. I remember hearing the first election results on the radio at Fighter Command. There were urgent demands for quiet from the gallant officers in their mess. 'The latest election figures,' said Alvar Liddell's golden voice from the wireless, 'Labour 123, Conservatives 88.' There was a terrible silence of disbelief, interrupted by a Wing-Commander with huge ginger whiskers culminating in spirals of hair on his cheeks, who blurted 'Try the Forces' programme', as though the figures there would be more sympathetic.

Demobilisation was a complicated bureaucratic business, finally ending in the distribution of a suit for every man at Olympia, with a vague regard for size, but none for taste or predilection. I was the recipient of a repellent brown number with tiny white dots, flung at me by an ill-tempered sergeant soured by the sight of so many potential victims escaping into civvy-street. The secrets of its manufacture were only revealed later when a spoilt Swedish brat set fire to my sleeve for fun, and bared a lining made of old pyjamas stitched together.

Never mind, it had been a hard war, and we had made-do and mended for so long that more than a grain of folly attended our reaction to peace, a peace which was for a long while nothing but a war without the shooting. Motor cars began to be produced again, all with shining headlamps. It was too soon for technical changes, but one small maker, ambitious for exports to other dilapidated countries, produced a glut of left-hand drive vehicles which nobody wanted. Oddly enough the company was saved, if not for long, by the sudden attention of cruising prostitutes, who snapped up all available models, since it suited their purpose to be on the pavement side as they crawled down Bond Street cajoling pedestrians. Private enterprise and initiative were returning. The thaw had set in. The land might yet be made into one fit for heroes. There was festival in the air. Optimism was the order of the day. Television blossomed to lighten our darkness. Far away, in Japan, the bomb had darkened the light, but it was a temporary darkening – an action taken to shorten the war. The United Nations, taken as seriously as it should have been by its 'founding fathers', was to be our steadying sail. We looked forward to the Fifties with impatience.

Peter Ustinov

Introduction

The Forties, reaping the bitter fruits of the previous decade, meant austerity – in dress, food, and a thousand other niggling restrictions that made life awkward. For the first five years, World War plunged the people of Britain into an alien world of evacuations and Anderson shelters, blackouts and sirens, silver barrage balloons and bombers. Churchill, the bulldog spirit in a siren suit, and Vera Lynn singing 'We'll meet again' symbolised the hopes of the nation. When victory came at last it had a sting in its tail, leaving the whole world stunned by the mushroom cloud that heralded the atomic age. The years of so-called peace that followed were marked by the same wartime bleakness and drudgery. Rebuilding was slow, there were few jobs for demobbed servicemen, and food rationing got even stricter. Britain became a welfare state, lost an empire, and painfully set about adjusting to her new place in the world.

The blitz brought out the true backs-to-the-wall spirit of the British. In 1940 *Vogue* wrote of 'whole chunks of the streets up everywhere and gaping ruins and rescue squads and choking dust (one gets *white* in London now, rather than black) and powdered glass tinkling about, and everyone being too, too normal . . .' Some people moved into hotels or at least sought the safety of their cellars for the evening in particularly bad raids. 'A recent alarm found the Dorchester shelter filling up with celebrities – several ministers without portfolios or gasmasks either, Lady Diana Cooper in full evening dress, Vic Oliver in serious mood, his wife Sarah Churchill asleep on the floor, and Leonora Corbett trying out a new hairdo.' Life went on in troglodite fashion: 'At the Dorchester, business booms, especially in the basement, where everyone spends the *alerte* being shampooed and set, and manicured, and massaged, and foam-bathed . . . Some shops, such as John Lewis, have canteen refreshments for bomb-bound customers. Austin Reed supplies books and magazines . . . Sampling the shelters and swopping experiences is still a good game.'

Lesley Blanch, *Vogue*'s feature writer, wrote of the dilemma facing Londoners as to whether to store their precious possessions or risk them – and lose them, as she did. Most people compromised. Lady Diana Cooper whittled her treasures down to three – a picture of her son, evacuated to America, a pair of candlesticks, and a portrait of her mother, the Duchess of Rutland, drawn by Queen Victoria. Cecil Beaton sent his Dalis and velvet curtains to the country but kept his desk, which had formerly belonged to Talleyrand, in London. Beaton took a series of photos for *Vogue*, showing the different, often beautiful face of London after five years of war: railingless squares, purple milkwort and ferns flourishing in the rubble, water repositories reflecting the trees, baseball in Hyde Park, and war exhibitions in bombed sites.

Country life was just as hectic as that of the town. 'Take my hostess,' wrote *Vogue*'s reporter in 1941. 'Her house is overflowing with relations and evacuees . . . an adenoidal, trancey under-house-maid will soon be her only standby. She is the local representative of the WVS; she organizes the Salvage Campaign for the village . . . She is secretary and treasurer to the Preserving Centre, and has to deal with the most complicated permits for sugar, fruit, etc. She grows all her own vegetables . . . attends ambulance classes, is a Voluntary County Organizer for the Women's Institute, helps run the Knitting Bee . . . and is now arranging that everyone who has hot baths going shall offer them to some of the troops billeted in plumbingless houses.'

People grumbled about wartime rudeness, and about shortages of essentials like razor blades and torch batteries. 'I wish the Board of Trade could release more elastic, before I lose the battle with Newton's Law of Gravitation,' wrote Lesley Blanch. Everyone bartered for goods, gave up their aluminium saucepans for Spitfires, and queued patiently for buses, cosmetics, food, and theatre tickets. The countryside was broken up into neat squares of allotments as people dug for victory. The thumbs-up sign became the wartime symbol of courage.

Food was topic Number 1. 'No-one dreams of settling the day's meals with the customary opening of what-shall-we-have-today? Even the most stubborn cooks know it's a case of what-can-we-get? And how shall we get it? Shall we fetch it by bus, on bicycle, or in a trap, a gig, a growler, or any of the odd assortment of vehicles now resuscitated to shame thoughts of petrol?' You never left home without a shopping bag, just in case you saw something worth buying on your way. Meals got simpler and smaller. 'Entertaining as a social obligation has gone,' wrote Cecil Beaton in 1942. 'It is nice to have two or six friends spend an evening together, to drink a bottle of wine, play chess, and eat apples. The apple has come into its own . . . There is a Biblical beauty in the way the housewife gets the best result from slender means.' The housewife, racking her brains at how to doll up potatoes, rice and pasta for the umpteenth time, might not have put it quite so poetically.

Nightlife continued vigorously, although some nights it was as likely to mean hours cooking in emergency field kitchens or driving ambulances through air-raids as dining, dancing, and theatre-going. Street placards bawled their double features: 'GIANT TANK BATTLE! FULL AMUSEMENT GUIDE!' In a feature called 'I'm just back from town,' in 1941, *Vogue* wrote: 'They're much more casual, socially, in London. Nothing is fixed up ahead . . . They wear *anything*. The faithful little black number, or a print dress, or even the suit they started out in at crack . . . There's no snob feeling about where you eat, or what or when. The Ritz Bar, or a Potato Bar (they've taken the place of Milk Bars and are stoutly sustaining). Restaurants are full up all the time; an endless chain of meals merging one into the next: lunch, tea, high tea, drinks, snacks, and dinner, all overlapping, and people neurotically demanding the oddest things, like cocoa.'

Although there was an official fixed price of five shillings a meal everywhere, some restaurants got round this with hefty cover charges. 'Many trimmings are added to food. Spam has assumed the sophisticated name of *Ham Americaine*; rabbit masquerades as chicken; and a shell heaped high with carrots and garnished with cabbage is still crab . . . Little inexpensive restaurants such as the Escargot, the Etoile, and the Quo Vadis are packed out. But so are such de luxe haunts as the Mirabelle; which might give Gibbon something to think about.'

Even love and marriage had to adapt to wartime circumstances. 'Time is of the essence of the contract. Leave is reckoned in days, hours, minutes. Dates are timed to the split second and girls no longer keep boys waiting. "Are you free next Wednesday, 4.30 to 8? I've special leave." "Can you lunch today?" "Can you

Artist's abri: when the siren sounds, the Ericksons rush to their farmhouse cellar at Senlis. In Eric's sketch, Mrs Erickson plays backgammon; their daughter knits; the Indo-Chinese servants stand with stiff respect and the poodle sleeps securely, 1940

marry me tomorrow?'" With two-day engagements and ten-days-leave honeymoons the norm, *Vogue* showed its readers how to get a wedding together in a week, and make the most of one's clothing coupons. 'Wedding cakes assume a surrealistic aspect, for since sugar-rationing, their icing façades have been replaced by satin covers, elaborately trimmed with lace frills, hand-painted bouquets, scrolls of silk cord, and embroidered in suitably felicitous phrases . . .' In 1940, at Penelope Dudley Ward's wedding to Private Anthony Pelissier, Fay Compton's son, both the bridegroom and the best man, John Mills, wore hairy khaki battledress with clumping army boots, 'looking at once splendid and forlorn in the undramatic practical accoutrements of modern warfare'.

Despite blitz- and bomb-damaged offices, *Vogue* continued to publish, although it cut back to a monthly basis, with fewer pages and a smaller print run due to the paper shortage. 'Don't be a dog in a manger about your *Vogue*,' the magazine stressed. 'Share it with your friends . . . When you've read it all, studied it and planned your outfits – pass it on to someone else.' Over the war years, *Vogue* became a unique record of history in the making, covering the home front with its characteristic wit and buoyancy, and even sending journalists like Lee Miller and Mary Jean Kempner to the front line to cover the war at first hand. It adapted its fashion coverage with an optimistic spirit to the stringencies of Purchase Tax, clothing coupons, and Utility clothes. From 1941 onwards, clothes rationing allowed you 66 coupons: a dress required 11, a skirt 7, shoes 5. '*Il faut* skimp, *pour être chic,*' wrote *Vogue*. 'Fashion is undergoing a compulsory course of slimming and simplification. If women must buy less, they will buy better.'

Austerity measures and their new lifestyles put women into tight, short-skirted Utility suits, slacks, wooden-soled shoes, and

<u>Above,</u> Harry W. Yoxall, *Vogue's* Managing Director, in his wrecked office after a near-by bomb explosion, 1940. <u>Opposite,</u> War Relief Ball at the New York Ritz, painted by Ludwig Bemelmans, 1941

practical turbans popularised by Clementine Churchill. Although there were many people who thought that women in uniform looked better out of it, uniforms for women had an irrevocable influence on fashion as the war dragged on. 'Polish yourself up,' wrote *Vogue*. 'Hair burnished and crisply cropped to the new length – it's a look that does not jar with uniform, with *women's* uniform. Somehow, more and more, the eye unconsciously measures women by this yardstick. Why does that shoulder-mane seem so out of date? Because it would look messy hanging on a uniform collar. What's wrong with those exquisite tapered nails? They couldn't do a hand's turn without breaking. The woman who can change instantly into uniform or munitions overalls and look charming, soignée, and right, is the smart woman of today.'

When silk stockings were banned in 1941 it was a bitter blow. 'Stockingless cream' was messy; bare legs were cold: 'Socks can contrive to look charming,' wrote *Vogue* hopefully, against a photograph of an elegantly dressed model wearing ankle socks. Lack of cosmetics also dashed morale. With only 25 per cent of the normal peacetime supply being manufactured, women had to save what they had for special occasions.

In the early months of 1940 there was still plenty of news from Paris. The Duchesse D'Ayen, one of the editors of French *Vogue*, reported that the Ritz Hotel now housed, among others, Lady Mendl, the Hon and Mrs Reginald Fellowes and their daughters, Elsa Schiaparelli and her daughter Gogo, Mrs Corrigan, the Sacha Guitrys, Major Metcalfe, Jean Cocteau, and Coco Chanel. The war broke down vigorous French formality and people enjoyed dropping in on each other. Lady Mendl and the Duchess of Windsor busied themselves with their war charity which sent packages of necessities from Versailles to needy soldiers. The glamorous Bal Tabarin nightclub, renowned for its snake dancer, was turned into a soup kitchen for out-of-work actors, who were waited on by the can-can dancers wearing white aprons.

When the Germans occupied Paris, Michel de Brunhoff, editor of *Vogue*, preferred to see his magazine suppressed rather than to collaborate with the enemy. Publication ceased for four years and news from France slowed to a trickle. Elizabeth Hoyt, an American woman living in Unoccupied France, sent a report during the winter of 1942: 'Your bicycle goes everywhere with you – on the back of the tram, down to the cellar, and up into your flat when you get home. There are bicycle taxis too, a trailer hauled by two men on bicycles in parallel or in tandem. One trailer I used was pulled *à la* rickshaw by a man who had no bicycle; it was marked *service rapide* . . . All life in France centres round the rationing restrictions . . . The stores and markets are full of Gestapo and special police agents, spying on the tradesmen and customers, and also on each other! The average monthly ration for an adult works out about like this – 16 ounces of cooking oil; 6 ounces of a watery, greasy liquid used for salad oil; 7 ounces of oleomargarine; 40 ounces of meat, including bone or fat; 8 ounces of imitation coffee; 35 ounces of sugar; 15 ounces of noodles or macaroni; 14 ounces of cheese; 15 ounces of dried vegetables; 4 ounces of jam; 36 ounces of potatoes; 15 pounds of bread; four bottles of wine; half a cake of imitation soap; one egg. All this isn't equal to one pound of food a day . . . There is no certainty that you will find the items or quantities to which you are entitled . . . For months during the first winter of German occupation I did not see a single potato or fresh vegetable in the markets . . . About the only thing you can buy without a ration ticket is a picture of Pétain.'

When the Allies retook Paris, *Vogue* was the first magazine to

be given permission to recommence publication. A joyful Liberation issue of 9,000 copies was printed, showing the latest fashions, on paper provided by the French Provisional Government from stock hoarded by the Germans.

Britain's own invasion came in the form of the GIs. From early in 1942, they wooed and won the war-weary British girls with their film-star accents and unlimited chewing gum, nylons, cigarettes, and Palmolive soap. *Vogue* encouraged its readers to help the American servicemen feel at home: 'Remember, everything is twice as much fun to these American boys if there's a girl in it . . . Frankness and informality are the keynotes to strike.' When the GIs left, the streets around Berkeley Square seemed strangely empty, although you could at last find a taxi in London again. When President Roosevelt died in 1945, Britain and indeed the whole world mourned as if for its own.

For Britain, victory heralded a slow and painful period of recovery which became known as the Second Battle of Britain. The country's trade deficit stood at £1,200,000,000. 'We work or want,' exhorted the street hoardings. Shortages continued and rationing of many foods, including meat, actually tightened, and did not finally end until 1954. There was still no petrol for pleasure driving. In addition, the winter of 1946–47 was the worst in Europe since 1870 and precipitated a fuel crisis, with power switched off for long periods during the day. The British, who had shown a good-humoured stiff upper lip when threatened by Hitler, got thoroughly fed up at the endless scrimping.

In June 1945 *Vogue* ran a nostalgic feature, 'What we want to have back': 'Our men . . . Our children – evacuated for safety; put in nursery schools because we were too busy with our war jobs to look after them . . . Sheer stockings . . . Wine, cheese, fruit . . . Fruit and more fruit . . . A rebuilt Queen's Hall . . . Evening décolletage . . . Scarlet buses: scarlet fire engines . . . Icecream sundaes: quantity and quality on the American scale . . . High heels, long evening dresses, silly hats, and all the gay nonsense that such a plenitude permits . . . Jewellers, clockmakers and shoemakers who will undertake repairs quickly and efficiently . . . Perfume . . . Fountain pens . . . Alarm clocks . . . Jersey fabrics . . . Four posts a day . . . Restaurant cars on the trains . . . Lingerie with lace and frills and fine handwork: austerity is particularly hard worn next to the skin . . . Easy telephoning – but was it ever? . . . Shoes . . . Corsets . . . Household furnishings: no matter, at first, how cheap, so long as they are gay, pretty and unrationed, to brighten our war-worn homes . . . Purchases tied up in paper and string – actually delivered if we wish . . . Sausages, the real thing . . . Loaded bookstalls . . . Flowers in flower-beds and cabbage banished to its proper place . . . Late running buses and trains . . . The commons and open spaces which Service- and other Ministries have borrowed from us, the public, for war purposes . . . A sea view, uninterrupted by concrete blocks, barbed-wire entanglements or grandstand scaffolding . . . Nourishing face creams . . . That forgotten phrase – music in our ears – "How many would you like?" . . .'

One of the few bits of excitement and glamour that brightened the general austerity was the wedding of Princess Elizabeth and Prince Philip of Greece at Westminster Abbey in 1947, followed the next year by the birth of their son, who was christened Charles Philip Arthur George.

For women the hardest pill to swallow was watching beautiful fabrics and clothes going for export only, while Sir Stafford Cripps, President of the Board of Trade, refused to remove clothing restrictions. Small wonder that when in 1947 Christian Dior launched his sensational, ultra-feminine New Look, women were putty in his hands. The New Look took up to twenty-five yards of luxurious fabric – velvet, brocade, furs, and lace – in a single skirt, hanging from a tiny waist. Princess Margaret adopted it immediately, and despite governmental outrage New Look clothes were a sell-out – wherever they could be found. Another new look that came to stay, and got smaller and smaller, was the bikini, the two-piece bathing suit incongruously named after a tiny Pacific atoll that was used for atom and hydrogen bomb tests by the US Army.

Six years of war had irrevocably altered the social climate of Britain. Much privilege was swept away, and extreme poverty had also vanished. In 1945 Winston Churchill's Coalition government was defeated by a landslide Labour victory under Clement Attlee. The Butler Education Act ensured a system of selective higher education, sowing the seeds of a future meritocracy, and in 1948 the Health Service Act, the National Insurance Act, and the Children's Act marked Britain's optimistic debut as a welfare state. 'The social conscience of the country has been growing steadily,' noted *Vogue*. 'The pessimist who regards progress as a myth finds no ammunition here.' Britain also began slowly dispossessing itself of its empire. India's independence in 1947 was hastened by the non-violent civil disobedience practised by Mahatma Gandhi and his followers. The following year Gandhi was murdered by a Hindu fanatic and a crowd of millions watched as the urn containing his ashes was cast into the sea near Bombay.

The war had also shown decisively what women were capable of. Without nannies – who were absent on munitions – they put

Above, a photograph of Gandhi taken just a few days before his death, showing his popularity not only with his followers, but with the general public, 1948. JOFFE. *Opposite,* HRH Princess Elizabeth, Duchess of Edinburgh, and Prince Charles, 1949. CECIL BEATON

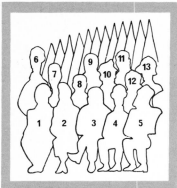

1, King George II of Greece; 2, Grand Duchess Charlotte of Luxembourg; 3, Mackenzie King, Prime Minister of Canada; 4, Generalissimo Chiang Kai-Shek of China; 5, Franklin D. Roosevelt, President of the USA; 6, King Haakon VII of Norway; 7, King Peter II of Yugoslavia; 8, John Curton, Prime Minister of Australia; 9, Peter Fraser, Prime Minister of New Zealand; 10, General Sikorski, Prime Minister of Poland; 11, Hubert Peirlot, Prime Minister of Belgium; 12, Eduard Benes, President of Czechoslovak Republic; 13, General Smuts, Prime Minister of the Union of South Africa

THE HEADS OF STATE of the TWENTY-SIX UNITED NATIONS . . . the free fighters of the world

COVARRUBIAS 1942

ALL ON OUR SIDE . . . here massed with their free flags . . . **PROUD ENEMIES OF THE AXIS**

their children into day-care and nursery schools and turned their hands to war work of every kind. By the end of the war, seven million British women were employed in the armed services or essential industry. After the war, French women were accorded the vote, although they still could not open a bank account without their husband's permission, and equal pay was a Utopian thing to come. The changing status of women found a frequent echo in *Vogue*. In 1946 Daphne du Maurier wrote: 'The birthrate is falling, and I know why, and so do all the other women of my generation. It has nothing to do with insecurity or atom-bombs or the movies. It is because we don't *want* a lot of children, and had the women of past generations known how to limit their families they would have done so . . . Why are the churches empty? Because, with modern warfare, hellfire holds no terror for us. And was it only fear of the hereafter that made my lady in her crinoline go to church three times on a Sunday? No, it was boredom.'

In 1947 Simone de Beauvoir, friend of Jean-Paul Sartre and one of postwar France's most incisive minds, neatly analysed the feminist dilemma in *Vogue*: 'Women are afraid that if they lose [their] feeling of inferiority they will also lose what gives them value in the eyes of men – femininity. The woman who feels feminine does not dare . . . to consider herself the equal of men. Yet, inversely, if a woman is stripped of her inferiority complex toward men, if she succeeds with brilliance in business, in social life, in her profession, she often suffers an inferiority complex in comparison to other women. She feels herself less charming, less amiable, less agreable because she is deprived of the femininity . . . Either [women] renounce in part the integration of their personalities, or they abandon in part their power of seduction over men.' *Vogue*, somewhat missing the point, called de Beauvoir 'a woman who thinks like a man'.

In America, 'teenagers' had also come into their own: for the first time adolescence was regarded as different from childhood. British mothers were filled with misgivings at this new and precocious breed, which wore makeup, participated in adult conversations, 'dated', earned a fortune babysitting after school, and ate revolting quantities of icecream. But *Vogue* saw no harm in such decadence: 'American youth is responsible as well as lively, and has many interests which our own might well emulate.'

Travel during the war generally meant blacked-out train corridors crowded with troops – 'every journey like peace-time bank holiday, but without the fun at the other end'. 'Is your journey really necessary?' asked the posters. 'The word holiday has dropped from our vocabulary,' wrote *Vogue* in July 1940, although just two months earlier it had naively promised, 'This summer you can still bake yourself golden brown on the beaches of the Riviera, see the superb scenery of the Pyrenees, stay along the Côte Basque . . .' For the duration of the war, practically the only taste of abroad in *Vogue*'s pages was in the photographs by Cecil Beaton, who went to Portugal, India, and China in his capacity as official war photographer. After the war, there were still currency restrictions to thwart you, but the British couldn't wait to pile into their cars and cross the Channel. Marghanita Laski wrote an ecstatic article from a 'pub' in Provence proving that two could enjoy fourteen days of French countryside, unrationed food, and sun for £40. 'We have just lunched off pâté and asparagus and andouillettes and a dish made of biscuits soaked in sweet white wine covered in chocolate and topped with grapes-in-brandy. In the distance a small hill is crowned with a sand-coloured Provençal village, an old castle four-square beside it . . . And all this for two guineas a day for

Opposite, the first peacetime voyage of the world's biggest liner, as seen by *Vogue*'s artist, René R. Bouché, 1946. *Above,* Mrs Henry Ford II drives – guess what? – a Ford, a green convertible, 1949. HERBERT MATTER

both of us.' Those who could afford to go further had their appetites whetted by articles on Sterling area destinations: Alec Waugh wrote on the West Indies and Ronnie Emmanuel on Cyprus.

The Thirties vogue for luxury cruises was resumed in 1945 when the *Queen Elizabeth,* which had already notched up sixty Atlantic crossings as a troopship, made her glamorous maiden voyage to New York. The following winter skiing got seriously under way again, with the usual crowd of royalty, celebrities, and brilliant skiers converging on St. Moritz, the women sporting the latest tight-fitting *fuseau* pants. In Colorado, a Chicago millionaire called Paepcke resurrected an old mining town called Aspen and turned it into a spanking new ski centre with the highest ski lifts and the most slopes in the country. Air travel began again. London's new airport at Heathrow was opened and for the first time ever you could buy a round-the-world ticket from one company, Pan Am. *Vogue* writer Allene Talmey and photographer Irving Penn did just that, and published the impressions of their trip in the magazine.

No new cars were manufactured in Britain during wartime, and petrol rationing forced people to put up with the old ones. America led the field in postwar car design, and popularised the shark's grin radiator, bulbous shape, and tail fins. 'Cars are reaching a state of perfect performance bordering on the monotonous,' wrote *Vogue* in 1949. 'Gone are the old nostalgic adventures (the very word "breakdown" is all but obsolete). Few even remember the days of hot geysers steaming from the radiator . . . Now, the mechanically half-witted can drive across the country, or meet the 6.08, sure that her car will get her there.'

Throughout the war, interior design and architecture remained pickled in aspic. 'We're all down to doll's houses,' noted *Vogue*, as people moved from ten rooms to two, or adopted a cavemanlike existence in their basements, or Anderson shelters when necessary. Syrie Maugham wrote a piece on 'Convertible rooms', explaining how to make the most of limited space with beds that turned into sofas and collapsible chairs. Even after the war, there wasn't much you could do to brighten up your home – if you still had one at all – with a £10 limit on decoration expenditure. The latest in postwar architecture was the prefab, which was built to last ten years. They sprang up like mushrooms on waste ground; with lace curtains and little gardens, the bombed-out British made them seem like home. The Festival Hall on London's South Bank, which was to become a bright inviting complex complete with Skylon at the 1951 Festival of Britain, was welcomed as an optimistic architectural renaissance. Its foundations were laid in 1949 and a time capsule within contained, among other things, a Benjamin Britten anthem, and a copy of *The Times*.

Industrial design was not Britain's strong point, and to overcome this the 'Britain can make it' exhibition opened at the Victoria and Albert Museum in 1946. Set up by the Council for Industrial Design, it was intended to display, both to the public at home and to markets abroad, the best of British design in everything that people could wear or use, including novelties such as 'personal' radio sets, folding cameras, and electric kettles. It was the Italians, however, who took the lead in postwar furniture design, using flexible, mobile pieces of furniture in a variety of materials, and daringly setting one style against another.

The cinema remained a favourite form of entertainment, although you could no longer buy icecream. People got tired of leaving during air-raids and seeing only half a film, and generally stayed put throughout the performance. Wartime programmes included not only the main feature, 'B' film, and newsreel, but also an official film made by the Ministry of Information, on topics such as food or salvage. British films improved out of all recognition with their sensitive portrayal of the war, while American films provided an escape from it, with cartoons like *Dumbo* and *Pinocchio* and jolly musicals starring Mickey Rooney, Betty Grable, Bing Crosby, Bob Hope, and Dorothy Lamour.

The theatre fared less well. People were unwilling to venture far from home, and wartime shows tended to run to comedies and classic revivals. Theatre designers found it a challenge to create costumes with the few coupons allocated to them. The Windmill never closed, but many theatres did, or dispersed to the provinces – many country dwellers felt that in this respect they had never been so lucky. The entertainment sensation of the decade was Danny Kaye, who was adored on both sides of the Atlantic.

ENSA provided entertainment of varying quality for both civilians and troops, while the Council for the Encouragement of Music and the Arts (CEMA) gave many people their first taste of opera, ballet, and symphony concerts. Independently founded in 1940, CEMA soon received government funding, and later became the Arts Council. After the war, the Edinburgh Festival of Music and Drama, the Shakespeare Festival at Stratford, which employed the talents of new producers Peter Brook, Anthony Quayle, and Walter Hudd, and the Aldeburgh Festival became highly successful cultural events outside the capital.

People amused themselves dancing the Conga and the Hokey Cokey ('as popular in Buckingham Palace as in Bermondsey') or tried to stay upright on the new ice rinks. But the most popular pastime was reading – whatever you could get your hands on. *War and Peace* became a best-seller, devoured by candlelight in the shelter. Unlike the First World War, this one produced no spate of idealistic war poets and writers. Instead there was *The Last Enemy* by reluctant hero Richard Hillary, a young Oxford-educated airman; Evelyn Waugh's satirical picture of the evacuees in *Put out More Flags;* and Norman Mailer's *The Naked and the Dead,* full of four-letter words, which the editor of the *Sunday Times* considered 'unfit for publication and especially unsuitable for any woman to read'. After the war, George Orwell's *Animal Farm* and *1984* painted a despairing view of Communism. Postwar France found solace in the philosophy of existentialism, propounded in the works of Jean-Paul Sartre, Albert Camus, and Raymond Queneau; this seemed to many outsiders to mean a rather shocking combination of unshaven, blackclad Bohemians, dark, jazz-filled coffee-bars, and general sexual and ethical freedom.

Radio was a lifeline uniting the British people throughout the war. By 1945 there were nearly 10 million wireless sets in Britain. There were news bulletins all day, instead of just in the evening. Newsreaders now introduced themselves, and the 'Forces' programme' became part of everyone's life. Everyone listened to J.B. Priestley's wartime chats, to *Workers' Playtime,* to *ITMA (It's That Man Again)*. On Sunday afternoons there was a good audience for *The Brains' Trust,* with philosopher Cyril Joad, who suggested that the answer to the woman surplus caused by the war was polygamy. The Third Programme was inaugurated 'for the alert and receptive listener' in 1946. 'It is news for Britain that culture should make news,' wrote Elizabeth Bowen in *Vogue*, noting that 'Britain's wavelength for intellectuals' had already aired Patrick Dickinson's *The Wall of Troy,* Laurie Lee's *The Voyage of Magellan,* and Louis MacNeice's *The Careerist.* 'It is high time that, in Britain, we had again what the Third Programme is not ashamed to stand for: a demand for the best . . . the Third Programme's perfectionism (as some see it) may be hard to take, may be antagonising, but it is bracing. Stress on style, manner, execution, virtuosity – can we in Britain, now, have too much of that?'

Television – or video, as it was often called – still had the aura of magic that radio had lost. 'This is television's decade,' wrote *Vogue* in 1940, when there were 3,000 sets in the United States. 'Television as a medium of entertainment will eventually kill sound broadcasting stone dead.' Although British television studios closed down for the duration of the war, Churchill's government appointed a committee to examine the future of television as early as 1943. By 1949, three and a half hours of programming were broadcast daily in Britain, and the unsightly 'H' aerials were a status symbol, while interior designers wondered how to disguise television screens in the drawing room. Val Gielgud, Dramatic Director of the BBC, discussed the implications of the new medium in *Vogue*. 'Video, even more than sound-radio, affects [listener-viewers] – in their own homes, and to a degree which is likely to condition to some extent the future of the civilised world. The control of radio is synonymous with Power . . . It is for the exercise of Power in combination with Responsibility that we must watch.'

For the average viewer, television was an optimistic symbol of progress as Britain faced the second half of the century, hopefully seeking a return to normality.

Opposite, Radio Hour in 1943, not a silent moment on the air! News and politics, humour and music, wait behind the turn of a button for everyone – to amuse, instruct, advertise, propagandise. Here we see Gertrude Lawrence, opening the new Revlon hour with Robert Benchley, Ray Milland, Moss Hart, 1943. BALKIN

Women at War

'This war effort could not have been achieved if the women had not marched forward in millions and undertaken all kinds of tasks and work for which any other generation but our own . . . would have considered them unfitted; work in the fields, heavy work in the foundries and in the shops, very refined work on radio and precision instruments, work in the hospitals, responsible clerical work of all kinds, work throughout the munitions factories, work in the mixed batteries . . . Nothing has been grudged, and the bounds of women's activities have been definitely, vastly, and permanently enlarged . . .

'In all this the women of Britain have borne, are bearing, and will continue to bear, a part which excites admiration among our Allies, and will be found to have definitely altered those social and sex balances which years of convention had established.'

From a speech by Winston Churchill to a gathering of 6,000 women in 1943.

Women – 'a luxury in peacetime,' wrote Lesley Blanch – played a vital part in time of war. The First World War had paved the way: it was conceded that women had done their bit, and were in fact worthy of their (considerably less) hire. In the Second World War, for the first time, they were marshalled and utilised to the full – 'soldiers without guns'. In addition to taking on countless jobs in factories and on the land, they joined the WVS, the Red Cross, the Home Guard, and the armed services.

Vogue's pages over the war years provide a record of women at war. Lesley Blanch wrote a series of unashamedly propagandist articles on the women's services 'on the job', stressing how women could be resourceful, dependable, brave, and willing to endure the rigours of service life without losing their femininity:

'Watch the ATS on the ack-ack gun-sites as night falls, shrilling their commands from range-finder to predictor, and on again to the gun crew. It's a dramatic setting: but long night watches can be undramatic to the point of dreariness in the uneventful icy silence of a black night . . . It's the same story with the searchlight batteries. Watch the girls lope out from their Nissen huts, like sleepy bears, in clumsy, shaggy topcoats, with curious kangaroo-pouched muffs to keep their hands warm . . .

'See the women of an emergency field kitchen, working by night, efficiently, stealthily, under battle conditions, cooking for hundreds, constructing ovens from baked mud, scooped clay, and old tins. They learn how to screen their ovens, how to build fires that send up no tell-tale smoke . . .

'Listen to the operational signal which brings the WAAF balloon crew diving out of their hut at the double – no, at the treble – to fly their balloon, to haul it down, or to bed it. Tough work, this, hauling and reeving; a question of experience or knack, more than sheer strength, say these women, whose sprawling charges brood over us protectively.

'Fine teamwork is apparent everywhere. Watch a Wren boat's crew bringing the Captain's launch alongside, shipshape and trim. It's dark and cold, and blowing great guns. Wrens work through the night in the repair docks, heaving the molten metal into moulds, or servicing the torpedoes. The prize worker on one night-shift had been a confectioner's assistant, doing the twiddly bits around the wedding cakes. Now, spanner in hand, she was zestfully tightening the last lethal-looking bolt.'

There was also the Air Transport Auxiliary – or ATA-girls, as they inevitably became known. This small band of pilots delivered fighters and bombers from factory to station, from station to maintenance unit. Commandant Pauline Gower, who had taken passengers for joyrides at air circuses before the war, started the ATA-girls with eight women who had flying certificates. Despite initial male prejudice that women would be unable to stand the strain of constant routine flights, they soon proved themselves as able as men to fly Spitfires, Hurricanes, and bombers (despite, as *Vogue* pointed out, being paid 20 per cent less). American air-speed record-holder Jacqueline Cochran, who ferried a bomber to Britain, wrote in *Vogue* of her 'tremendous, unreasonable pride' when she saw the WAAFs and ATA-girls, 'because they were so capable, so casually brave, so gay, and yet so responsible. I was proud because they were women doing the same work as men, and doing it well . . . I was amused and delighted to hear that the women who made the best mechanics in the maintenance and repair units (and, on the especially delicate instruments, were found to be better than men) were those who knew how to embroider and do needlework.'

The Women's Land Army played an equally crucial role. By 1942 there were 36,000 full-time Land Girls in Britain, learning every aspect of farmwork, planting vegetables in the flowerbeds of Britain's stately homes, and cultivating downlands for crops. In addition, to cope with seasonal pressure, there were the WELCs – the Women's Emergency Land Corps – local village women from manor house, shop, and cottage who worked in gangs, harvesting or planting, and earned 11d an hour – 'and earn is the word'.

The everyday sight of women in uniform took some getting used to, although Peter Quennell, writing in *Vogue*, confessed that he found them neither shocking nor surprising, nor even unbecoming: 'When, after all, have they worn anything else?' Lady Louis Mountbatten, Chief Superintendent of the St John Ambulance, was reported to dine out frequently in her chic uniform.

Many ladies enrolled in the caring professions, as nurses, VADs, or in the Red Cross. The Duchess of Kent headed the Wrens, the Duchess of Gloucester the WAAFs. *Vogue* saluted them all, and asked in 1945: 'Where do they go from here – the Service-women and all the others, who without the glamour of uniform, have queued and contrived and queued, and kept factories, homes, and offices going? Their value is more than proven: their toughness where endurance was needed, their taciturnity where silence was demanded, their tact, good humour, and public conscience; their continuity of purpose, their submission to discipline, their power over machines . . . all the things men liked to think women couldn't be or do . . . How long before a grateful nation (or anyhow, the men of the nation) forget what women accomplished when the country needed them? It is up to all women to see to it that there is no regression – that they go right on from here.'

Right, Princess Elizabeth, honorary Colonel of the Grenadier Guards, wearing the grenade of the regiment in her cap, 1943. Her diamond brooch of the regimental badge was subscribed for and given to her by the officers and men. When her father appointed her to the post the previous year, the senior regiment of footguards had a woman colonel for the first time in its history.

'SALUTE TO THE SENIOR SERVICE': The Wrens, 'Never at Sea', went to sea at last. <u>*Far left, above,*</u> Lady Cholmondeley, Staff Officer at WRNS Headquarters, shown against her portrait by Sargent, 1940. In the previous war she had been a WRNS volunteer. 'In private life she loves pictures, music, the theatre, her houseful of treasures; is a great friend of Toscanini.' <u>*Far left, below,*</u> 'the Wren type', 1941. According to Lesley Blanch, 'the Wren has a serenity, even a faint austerity, a balanced detachment; a quietness which is not dull, a dignity which is not pompous . . . I hasten to add they are pretty and feminine, as well-groomed and well-dressed, and as concerned with complexion, manicure, and hairdressing as any other women, in or out of uniform.' <u>*Left,*</u> Wren recruits swarming down from the quarter boom 'somewhere on a loch', 1943. The Wrens had to learn to do it in thirty seconds, like their male counterparts. <u>*Above,*</u> Wrens dining at Greenwich, 1941. CECIL BEATON. <u>*Right,*</u> 'the rope trick, Wren style', 1943. LEE MILLER

<u>WE'RE IN THE ARMY NOW:</u> Ack-Ack, ATS and WAACs. *Far left, above,* 'the WAACs are pretty' . . . Toni Frissell's photograph, taken for *Vogue,* was adopted by the US Government for the cover of the official WAAC recruiting bro-chure, 1943. *Far left, below,* the Ack-Ack mixed batteries line up on the gun-sites for the day's practice. CECIL BEATON. *Far left, below centre,* mixed gun teams at the range finder, 19[ ] LEE MILLER. *Left,* the searchlight battery girls stand at ease sing, 1943. LEE MILLER. *Top,* HRH the Princess Royal [ ] ATS Commandant Jean Knox, 1942. *Above,* ATS lorry c[ ] drivers study their route, 1942

WOMEN IN THE AIR: ATA-girls, WAACs, and WAVES. _Right,_ a Polish woman pilot flying a Spitfire for the ATA, 1942. _Below,_ American ace airwoman Jacqueline Cochran, holder of 17 speed records, ferried a bomber to Britain and wrote an article for _Vogue_ on her impressions of the ATA-girls and WAAFs, 1941. She sent her fee to the Spitfire fund. TONI FRISSELL. _Centre right,_ WAAFs servicing a barrage balloon from the inside, 1941. CECIL BEATON. _Far right, above,_ Anne Douglas of the ATA climbs into her Albacore. LEE MILLER. _Far right, below,_ WAVES overhauling a plane, 1943. LOUISE DAHL-WOLFE

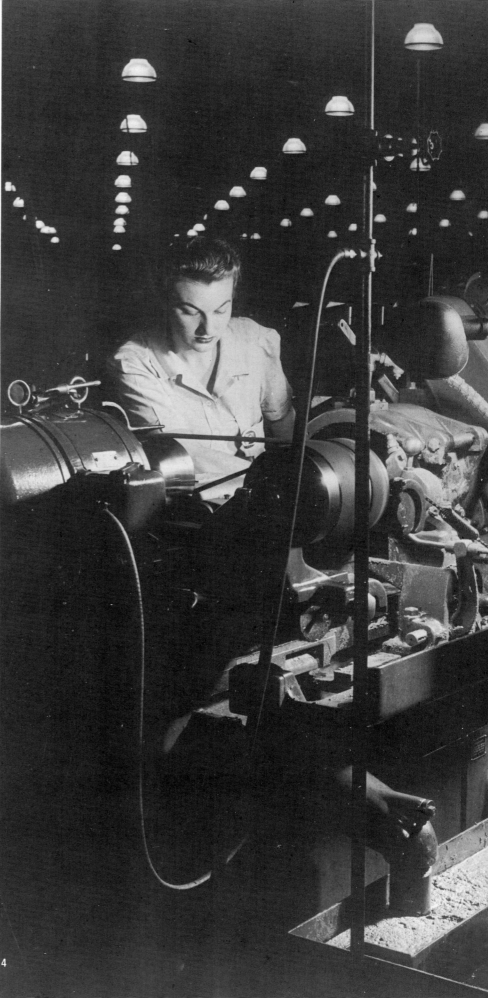

Working as a part-time saleswoman, releasing a younger unmarried woman for munitions

HELP WANTED

At a factory which produces aeroplanes and tank parts; this doctor's wife is working a daily part-time shift of four hours

Volunteers bind and repair books for the hospital and service libraries

One volunteer does agricultural work. The other brings out her midday meal

In a British restaurant, some of which are organized and run by the W.V.S., volunteers serve communal meals

Standing-by on duty, civil Defence Workers make camou-flage, threading the netting with different coloured tapes

The Home Defence Corps learn to be useful in an invasion. This unofficial women's Home Guard meets in the evening

5

WOMEN AT WORK ON THE LAND AND IN THE FACTORIES: _1,_ girls of the Land Army learning traditional agricultural crafts such as thatching, 1943. LEE MILLER. _2,_ WELCs hoeing upland cabbages in traditional formation, 1942. _3,_ Mrs William Hoppin, Land Army head for Farmington, Connecticut, learning to drive a tractor, 1942. _4,_ two of the three-quarter million American women now in the war industry, here running grinding machines, making propellers, 1942. LOFMAN. _5,_ 'Help wanted – female': *Vogue* shows the jobs women are needed for, 1942

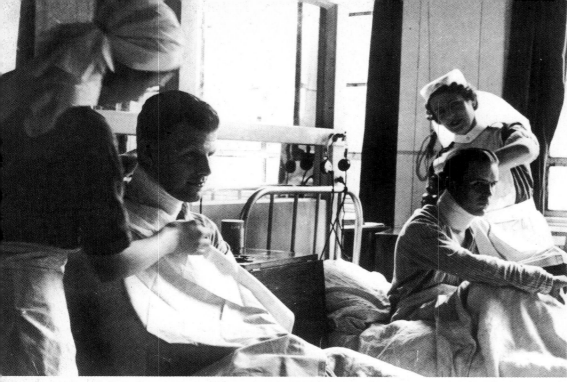

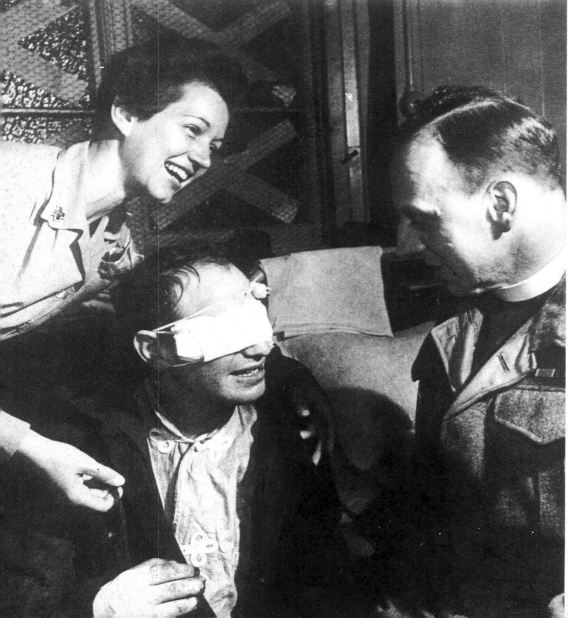

SISTERS OF MERCY: *Top left,* nurses care for the victims of war. *Left,* a Red Cross worker and a padre comfort a wounded American soldier, 1943. TONI FRISSELL. *Top,* Lady Louis Mountbatten, Chief Superintendent of the St John Ambulance, 1945. *Above,* actress Dorothy Hyson does part-time VAD nursing between performances of *Under One Roof,* 1941. *Right,* mosquito-netted operating room of an evacuation hospital in Normandy; a contrast of white to concentrated light, and khaki shadows, 1944. LEE MILLER

Letter from Paris

BY **BETTINA WILSON**, *Vogue* Fashion Representative

Paris in the fourth month of the war is an attractive, comfortable, almost normal city with a quasi-country charm. Although you can enjoy such luxuries as smart hats and taxis, nobody will look at you askance if you go hatless or ride your bicycle. Hospitality in the home has practically become a cult. You eat simple two-course lunches or dinners in private houses, and you go back to someone's house after the theatre and eat scrambled eggs with champagne substituting for coffee. The war seems to have weakened, if not completely broken down, the hitherto impregnable barriers of French formality.

There is an allied flavour to the uniforms, with English Army, Navy, and Air Force officers passing through; and with lots of Polish aviators in bluish-grey waiting to be sent to join English squadrons. Young RAF flyers on their first Paris leaves sit in every *boîte,* tapping out rhythms to the tantalising music. These boys are refreshing, but heart-breaking – with their infantile faces.

Paris is beginning to open up a little at night, to take care of the 'leave' exuberance. However, nightclubs throw you out bodily at eleven, leaving you nowhere to go. Theatres are opening, and nearly every opening is a benefit performance. Noel Coward arranged a benefit performance of *Spring Fever* with a French cast. It was a huge success and continues to play to full houses.

Maurice Chevalier belongs at the Casino de Paris. It's his atmosphere. He is exactly the right entertainment for the war; he is human, he's funny, he's touching, and he adores his audience.

The only places where you can hear music are Scheherazade, the Boeuf sur le Toit and the Elysées Bar, where the sensational 'Môme' Piaff sings. She is the new war songstress. She belongs to that hoarse-throated, loose-hair-over-the-eyes school of French singers. Her best records are '*C'est lui que mon coeur a choisi*' and '*Je n'en connais pas la fin.*'

The moment the military element turned up in Paris, women began wishing they had ordered less practical clothes. The men clamour for attractive, almost frivolous clothes and definitely want you to wear dinner-dresses at night.

The strangest activities go on at the couturiers. Creed keeps a whole *atelier* working on children's clothes for evacuated children. The little models are captivating, made out of all the odds and ends of fine Creed woollens with all the Creed technique and finesse. They would sell for shocking prices, but he gives them all to Isabel Kemp's organisation to distribute in the evacuated districts. They certainly will educate the younger generation to Paris smartness! Captain Molyneux keeps his salesgirls and workrooms busy knitting for the soldiers when work is slack. In fact, when you go into any of the couture houses, there is a knitting-bee atmosphere.

One of our favourite Paris wartime stories is about the fate of the magnificent furniture of the Lopez-Willshaws. Some of it originally came from the Palace of Versailles, and most of it is of museum quality. Mr Lopez, with a thought for posterity, willed the best of it to the Louvre. The first week of the war, a huge van drew into the Lopez courtyard, and instructions from the curator of the Louvre were presented to the butler to the effect that they had come to rescue their property. The furniture was packed and driven away to be hidden in the country until after the war, leaving the huge salons of the magnificent Louis XIV house bare.

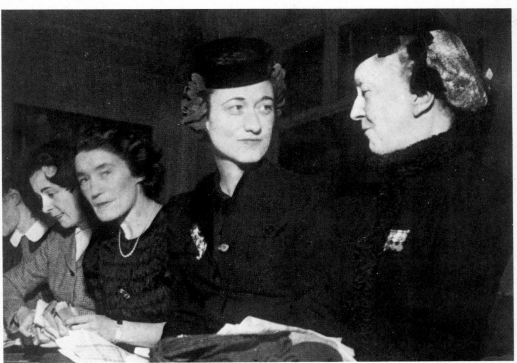

Left, the blacked-out Place Vendôme, 1940. BRASSAI. *Above,* the Duchess of Windsor and Elsie Mendl busy with their war charity, 1940. *Below left,* Parisian wartime gathering: M. Dali, M. Cocteau, Mlle Chanel, Mme Dali, M Samosa, 1940. AGNETA FISCHER. *Below right and Bottom right,* the Bal Tabarin, now turned into a fashionable soup kitchen, 1940. SCHALL. *Bottom left,* a 'cycling taxi', 1940.

Americans at War

'America is going flat out to help Britain,' wrote *Vogue* in 1941. 'Clark Gable's popularity pales beside that of Winston Churchill, whose fighting speeches and epigrams are quoted enthusiastically . . . There are no more large private parties – only "Help Britain" benefits in all their many guises.' There were also countless benefit dinners in smart restaurants which raised thousands of dollars for needy causes such as Funds for France, the Care of European Children, and the Musicians Emergency Fund.

The Bundles for Britain shop on ritzy Park Avenue sold wool, accepted and distributed clothing, and made surgical dressings to send overseas. Socialites like Mrs John Sims Kelly, the former debutante Brenda Frazier, turned their energies to Navy Relief, and Mrs Dwight Morrow worked for the USO War Apppeal. Gertrude Lawrence, appearing on stage in New York, sewed pyjamas for soldiers between performances.

In 1942, when the United States entered the war, Americans began to experience hardship at first hand. Mrs Roosevelt, the President's wife, visited Britain to study the immense field of women's war work. New York, whose lights were normally visible sixty miles at sea, got used to a 'dim-out' rather than a real blackout. The Breakers, the magnificent Newport 'cottage' built by Cornelius Vanderbilt, was thrown open to all as a public air-raid shelter. Suddenly New York nightclubs and restaurants, traditionally dead in summer, were full of uniformed men and their girls in evening dress, and offered special rates and the best tables for servicemen. There was even tea-dancing at the Stork Club.

Above right, Bundles for Britain shop, Park Avenue, 1941. *Right,* American fundraisers at 'Benefits': Mr Condé Nast *(left),* 1941; Mrs Morton Schwartz and Prince Serge Obolensky *(right),* 1940. *Below,* New York, usually dimmed-out, under practice black-out, 1942. *Opposite,* servicemen's lounge, Grand Central Station, 1944. ERIC

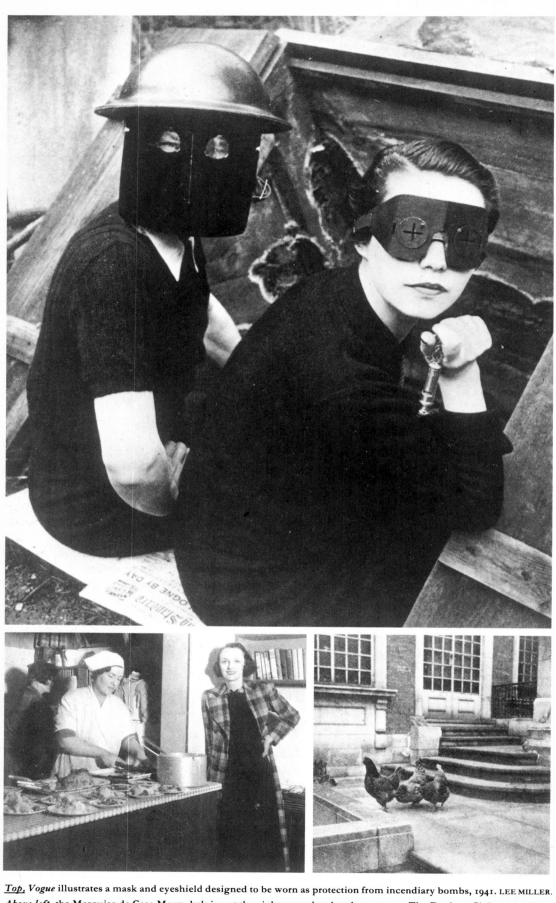

Top, Vogue illustrates a mask and eyeshield designed to be worn as protection from incendiary bombs, 1941. LEE MILLER.
Above left, the Marquise de Casa Maury helping at the eightpenny hot-lunch counter at The Feathers Club, 1941. _Above right,_ chickens living off the land in Mayfair, 1945. _Right,_ Virginia Woolf's bomb-sliced home leaves Duncan Grant's and Vanessa Bell's murals on public view, 1941

London Life

JANUARY, 1942

All life is now lived in suitcases. Emergency snatch cases stand by our beds, lilos, hammocks, or wherever we sleep: everyone goes around carrying suitcases for the night, plus their dearest treasures – maybe favourite clothes, a *batterie de beauté,* a packet of love letters, or the family jewels. Taxis being incalculable, and trains more so, the luggage-lugger has to decide between staggering under her all or travelling light and free, but risking a return to nothing but demolition squads at work in the remnants of the area. 'Safe as houses' now seems an obsolete phrase, and in rather poor taste, too.

Dinner guests must, of course, be bedded down – in the dining room, in the basement. People arrive early, hoping to cadge a bath before dinner and the blitz. This has done away with all that tiresome entertaining of semi-friends and near bores. One only invites those one really wants to see. 'Come in and have a bath,' rather than a drink, is the new social gesture – soap and hot water being a far more pleasing offer than any amount of gin and lime, scotch and soda. Many have had to master the dry-clean necessitated by bombed hot-water systems. Some swear by eau de Cologne or friction lotions; others rely on cold creams. (Hairdressers carry on with tin basins and kettles laboriously boiled on oil stoves.) There are surprising shortages. 'D'you mind cleaning your face on a towel, darling,' cries the harassed hostess, who finds it easier to pay laundry bills than lay hands on face tissues.

Thrifty householders have planted their window-boxes with mixed herbs. Most people have moved down, basementwards, and assembled all their dearest possessions in one cluttered, cosy living room, with a welcoming jumble of books, pictures and needlework and drinks and plants and photographs – thus saving heat and light. The many enforced separations have produced a spate of these personal belongings once more. ('That's one of her after she reached Montreal, the poppet.')

Those who are not kept from their own hearth by time bombs find plenty to occupy their scant leisure. The daily maid scuttles home before the 'sireens', and many wives and some husbands set to in the kitchen. Useless to excel at one or two exotic dishes, and show off over soufflé or zabaglione, for no meal can be planned ahead. You take what you can get, and make what you can of it, very often having to cook on an open fire, too. Onions being as scarce as peaches, even the most elegant cook can no longer baulk at hot-pots or stews as dinner-party fare. Cooking is now a major topic of conversation, and beating the blitz to it; explicit experts being as strenuously avoided as bomb-bores.

London's big hotels are crowded out. They have acquired the air of luxury liners, passengers signing on for a night's voyage or longer, for an endlessly protracted, portless voyage. Others go to dine and stow away for the night, caught by a particularly violent barrage. Overhead, the searchlights stab through the murky London night; the guns bark out, their pale icy flashes light the scene, which is – yes – pretty, with the golden sparkle of shell bursts. There is the uneven sinister sound of planes overhead, the heaving impact, the crunch and roar of a bursting bomb . . . the sudden slackening of nervous tension . . . 'M'm, yes that was a near one . . .' The roof-spotter's bell rings out in warning; some take cover, some continue to dine and dance. '

Back to the Land

Food and petrol rationing and no servants soon put paid to the idle weekending which had previously constituted country life. Country women and many Londoners immersed themselves in the rural war effort, digging furiously for victory or turning their big houses into hospitals and evacuation centres. Mrs John Betjeman became self-sufficient in Berkshire. She managed without petrol by training her Arab pony Moti to draw a dog cart in which she shopped, met guests, and cheerfully drove nine miles to lunch. Helped by two evacuee schoolmasters, she looked after her own big vegetable and herb garden, and kept British Saanen goats, which she milked twice a day. She also rode the dawn parachute patrols on the downs.

Londoner Lady Diana Cooper, with a capital outlay of £50, singlehandedly and energetically ran her own three-acre farm before accompanying her husband Duff Cooper to Singapore. The outstanding beauty of her generation, Lady Diana was no Marie Antoinette; she kept chickens, pigs, goats, a cow, and bees. *Vogue* reported that she buckled to work at 6.30 am to milk the Jersey cow Princess; then after feeding the animals she rushed to get through the various jobs such as collecting swill from neighbours, cheesemaking, and cutting hay, before feeding and milking again at sunset.

Vogue photographer Norman Parkinson and his fashion-model wife Thelma, helped by their ten-year-old daughter Jennifer, also turned to farming at Bushley in Gloucestershire. Parks wrote: 'Twice weekly we collect pig swill in the trailer . . . Hotels, cafés, and the cinema have bins with *Parks' Pig Food* on the lid . . . At first hotel managers were a little surprised that we should collect the bins from the back door at four, and return for dinner by the front at eight. "Leave plenty on the side of your plate," we remind each other. "More for our pigs."'

Top, threshing wheat on Parkinson's farm, and *above*, Parks collecting pig swill in 'Snort', 1944. *Right*, 'Ancestral hall or no, the terrace must have more manure.' Drawing by Marshall, 1940. *Facing page, above left*, Lady Diana Cooper in sombrero and peasant kerchief on her home farm, 1941. CECIL BEATON. *Above right*, Mary Churchill shouldering a stook at Breccles Hall, Norfolk, 1940. CECIL BEATON. Below, Mrs John Betjeman and goats, 1940. RAWLINGS

Away from Home

Autumn 1939 saw the first wave of evacuees leaving the cities for the country. P.L. Travers, author of *Mary Poppins,* wrote poignantly in *Vogue* of railway station separations. 'The land of our fathers becomes the land of our children,' wrote *Vogue,* next to photographs of evacuees wandering lost and bewildered around country houses. Wilton House, which had been a hospital in the First World War, became home to 40 little children from Kentish Town. But vast gardens, regular baths, and green vegetables were not always appreciated by city children, while their fosterparents were nonplussed at bedwetting, vermin, and demands for pie and chips. 'Hopes that evacuation would have a softening effect on slum children and Mayfair hostesses have been in both cases largely unrealised,' wrote Marghanita Laski. By January 1940, all but 600,000 of the million and a half evacuees had gone home.

Better-heeled children were sent to America. By late summer 1940, more than 2,000 children had already landed in the United States, although this option came to an end after the sinking of the 'City of Benares' with the loss of 73 children. English children were reported to display an endless curiosity about things like drugstores, baseball, tomato juice for breakfast, station wagons, and banana splits, and could broadcast home over the radio on 'Friendship Bridge' on Tuesdays at four.

Opposite, dignity and impudence – a small evacuee explores the huge grounds of Wilton House, 1940. *Above left,* a different sort of evacuee: away from the dangers of bombing, statues from the palace at Versailles are safe in the grounds of a château in the Touraine, 1945. *Left,* drill squads on the green, paratroops, and evacuees bring the war home to English villages, 1940. FRANCIS MARSHALL. *Above,* overseas evacuation: 'No. 404 wants to bring his white mice aboard', 1940. FRANCIS MARSHALL

Exodus

BY LEE ERICKSON

We did not dare look back at the house. As we turned into the only road left open, we joined a slowly moving mass of carts, farm wagons, lorries and cars piled with bedding and families; refugees on foot, some women with thin shoes worn through, stumbling along on swollen, bleeding feet, pushing perambulators, pulling carts, carrying babies, dragging exhausted children by the hand.

They had come from the North, from Picardy, from Flanders; they had been walking two days, three days, a week; they had eaten little, slept in fields, lain in ditches as the airplanes machine-gunned the road. They didn't know where they were going.

Flight is too swift and easy a word to describe so dreadful a thing as this. Exodus is better – slower, heavier, more painful. This sluggish river of tragedy filled the road as far as the eye could see. It was moving slowly along all the lovely roads of France in the bright sunshine, like slowly flowing blood.

In the four hours and a half that it took us to reach Paris, I saw only one woman weeping.

There was a lost dog running frantically among the wheels; further on, he found his master, a lone, old man wheeling a bicycle, the seat of his pants worn through. Someone gave him a rope, and with trembling hands he tied his dog to the handlebars to keep him safe.

Near Chantilly there was an alert. The sirens screamed, the guns boomed, there was the humming drone of German planes. Like one mass, the refugees scattered under the trees and under the wagons. At the all-clear signal, they went on as before, their expressions unchanged.

A few hours after we left Senlis, a bomb fell thirty yards from our house and blasted our doors and windows across the rooms. The wife, mother and daughter of our butcher were killed. The butcher has gone mad. All our little tradesmen are homeless.

BY THOMAS KERNAN

We fled the length of France before the advance of the German armies. Bordeaux was triple its size with refugees. Deserters filled the streets. Food was running short. No rooms were to be had.

On British warships, journalists Pertinax, Harry Knickerbocker, Eve Curie, Geneviève Tabouis took the road to exile. But for most Americans, Dutch, Belgians, Czechs, Poles, there was no means of escape at Bordeaux, and we fled down the coast to Bayonne, Biarritz, Saint-Jean de Luz.

At Saint-Jean de Luz, you can go no further. There is only the Atlantic, and the barricaded frontier of Spain. It is land's end.

The bay of Saint-Jean in June should be bright and smiling, with white villas on green mountainsides and fishermen's boats painted kingfisher-blue. But from June 20 to 24, there roared in a storm such as even Biscay has rarely produced. Thousands of men, women and children cowered without shelter on the drenched docks of Saint-Jean. Trucks and trains arrived every hour with a thousand more. The British Navy again came to the rescue, and in three days of howling tempest embarked all the phantom governments, the lost causes, the gallant and ghostly hopes of Europe.

Sikorsky and twenty thousand of the Polish Army who fled

Above, 'sleeping at night, exhausted, on the pavements, in the rain . . .' BENITO.
Opposite, the exodus of the Ericksons from Senlis, 1940. ERIC

across Lithuania and Norway to France now fled again to England. The prince-consort of Holland with the general staff of the Dutch Army took their turn in the open fishing-boats through rain and waves to the big ships. The dissenting government of Belgium, the exiled embassies and officers of Czechoslovakia, belated Englishmen, personalities of Norway, all waited on the pavements in the rain.

Four great steel-grey liners waited in the roads, hardly visible in the mist. The fishing-boats chugged back and forth, bucking wind and sea. The convoy slipped off for England in the dawn of the twenty-fifth, just as the storm began to calm.

Saint-Jean was bathed with late afternoon sun on the twenty-seventh, when three hundred blond young German giants arrived to garrison the town. Within ten minutes, the French girls were flirting with them, asking that their photos be taken with the omnipresent Leica; the children were fingering the motorcycles; the men, even those still in uniform, were offering cigarettes to the conquerors.

Captain Edward Steichen

Thérèse Bonney

Lee Miller

Mary Jean Kempner

Katherine Blake

Left, troops enter Burma, 1945.
CECIL BEATON

Vogue at War

In the early years of the war, *Vogue* concentrated on helping women adjust to their new roles – coping on the home front with evacuee children, rationing, and absent menfolk, or joining up themselves. However, as the war progressed, and particularly when victory was in sight, if distant, *Vogue* brought the battlefront into readers' lives. Suddenly the magazine took on a completely different look, with dramatic, savage, heart-touching pictures of war and all its faces, often used full-page for impact. Some were agency pictures, but many were exclusive to *Vogue*. 'No previous happening in the history of man has produced a visual record comparable to that made by the photographers of World War II,' wrote photographer Edward Steichen in *Vogue*. For a few years, *Vogue* itself built up a unique impression of the war through the extraordinary pictures and personal impressions of its own war reporters, photographers, and artists.

One of *Vogue*'s most prolific reporters was the American photographer Lee Miller, who had learnt her craft from Man Ray. She was with the American Army from D-Day onwards, often as the only woman correspondent, and sent back exclusive eyewitness reports and photographs. She saw the freeing of France (in Paris she was hailed as the *femme soldat*), Belgium, and Alsace, hitch-hiking her way round to record US tent hospitals in Normandy, the siege and assault of St Malo, German surrenders on the Loire, and refugees trailing back into Luxembourg after its liberation. She accompanied a column of North African soldiers trudging through the snow toward the Rhine, and entered Cologne on the heels of the capturing US Army, climbing a tower on the Hohenzollern Bridge to take shots across the river while the Germans were still using the east bank towers as observation posts. She went to Buchenwald and Dachau. 'Believe it,' she wrote. 'No question that German civilians knew what went on. Railway siding into Dachau camp runs past villas, with trains of dead and semi-dead deportees. I usually don't take pictures of horrors. But don't think that every town and every area isn't rich with them. I hope *Vogue* will feel that it can publish these pictures.' *Vogue* did.

On to Frankfurt, Nuremberg, and then Munich. Lee Miller was living in Hitler's apartment there when the Führer's death was announced, taking a bath in his bath and having a nap in Eva Braun's bed at her flat a few streets away. She was the first correspondent to arrive at Berchtesgaden, and photographed the Eagle's Nest, set ablaze by the departing SS: 'In the morning, the fire was nearly out and so were the looters, in force. Everybody hunted for souvenirs of Life with Hitler and explored the miles of underground living quarters cut into the rock under and behind the house. Miles of library, dining rooms, cinema machinery, living rooms and kitchen space. Rustic Bavarian furniture and heavy art pottery were the style of decoration. Cases of silver and linen with the eagle and swastika above the initials AH found their way into the pockets of the souvenir hunters and the books were tossed around if they didn't have a book plate or dedication or personal-looking binding. It was like a very wild party with champagne corks whizzing over the flagpole and the house falling down over our ears . . . There isn't even a piece left for a museum on the great war criminal . . . and scattered over the breadth of the world are forever going to be shown a napkin ring or a pickle fork, supposedly used by Hitler . . .'

Another *Vogue* staffer, Cecil Beaton, was employed by 'Minnie', the Ministry of Information, to record the war. Despite feeling a fish out of water at first – his previous assignments had been reporting on the social round and taking society portraits – he produced some of the most dramatic and immediate images to come out of the war: world-famous pictures of bomb damage in London, fighting in the jungles of Burma, and the strange, surreal shapes of wreckage in the Western Desert.

Vogue also had reporters in the Pacific. Mary Jean Kempner wrote of the loneliness of the GIs still fighting on after the V-E celebrations, and visited troops wounded at Iwo Jima in hospital in Honolulu. Also at Iwo Jima, where thousands of Americans died, was Captain Edward Steichen of the US Navy. One of the world's great photographers, who had worked extensively for *Vogue* before the war, Steichen was Director of the Navy Photographic Institute and of Navy Combat Photography. He was aboard the aircraft carrier *Lexington* when it was torpedoed and was awarded the Distinguished Service Medal. He sent back copy and a picture of an endless field of white crosses on Iwo Jima, and selected some of the great war photographs for *Vogue* to publish.

Other *Vogue* staffers also joined up and sent back their impressions of their new lives. Photographer Arik Nepo became a *poilu* in the French Army and was billeted in a barn. ('When all's said and done, straw isn't bad stuff. One can get used to anything.') Irving Penn, rejected by the Army because of a heart condition, joined the American Field Service, and photographed the ravages of war in the Apennines and at Anzio. Lydia Sherwood, editor, and niece of Robert Sherwood, Bettina Wilson, fashion editor with French *Vogue*, and Katherine Blake, American *Vogue*'s hostess editor, all joined the Red Cross and were sent to North Africa.

Some of the most harrowing photographs to appear in *Vogue* were taken by Thérèse Bonney, an American journalist who like her friend Gertrude Stein had adopted France as her home. She was the only photographer with carte blanche at the Battle of France, and gained the Croix de Guerre, the Legion d'Honneur, and the Finnish White Rose for her heroic rescue work. Her pictures of children, exhausted and terrified, refugees and orphans, reveal immediately who are the ultimate sufferers in war.

Polish-born *Vogue* illustrator Feliks Topolski was sent by the British government to sketch in Italy, Africa, Burma, India, China, Russia, and England, and many of his drawings appeared in the magazine. Another *Vogue* artist, René Bouché, visited Frankfurt at the end of 1945 and sketched his impressions of black markets and fraternisation between GIs and Fräuleins. 'The sidewalks were piled ten feet high with rubble, the houses were ebony ruins, but the people were ideologically untouched. They acted as if they had survived an earthquake, not lost a war . . .'

Nada Patcévitch, once a member of *Vogue*'s staff and the wife of the president of Condé Nast, went to Berlin after the war and paid a visit to Hitler's bunker. 'Once the walls had been panelled in wood and the furniture covered in blue velvet. Now the cement from which the wood had been ripped was scratched with Russian names, and only a few torn shreds of velvet clung to the broken springs of a sofa. It was damp and musty-smelling. One shivered with cold and the unpleasant suspicion that all the terror and frustration – the horror of that place – still hung in the air.'

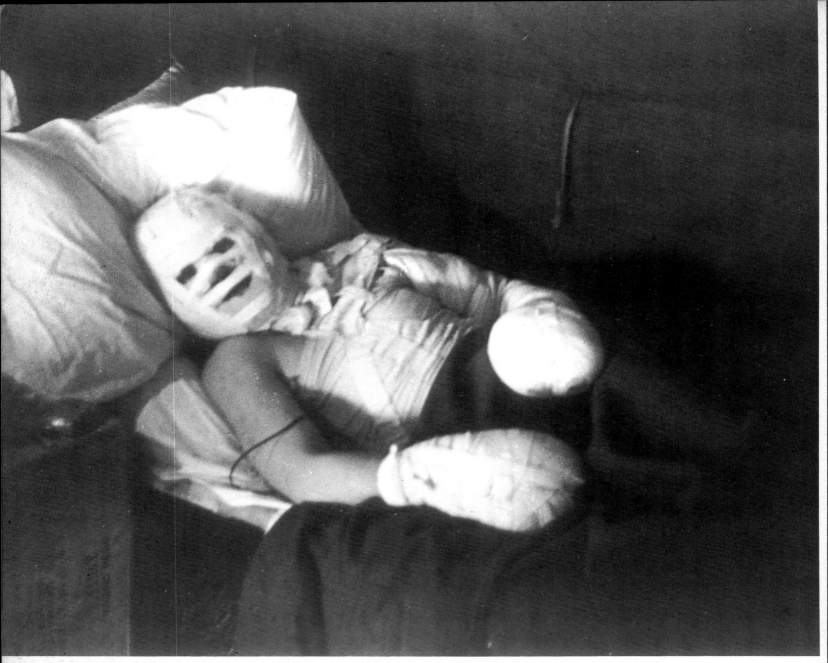

'A BAD BURN CASE ASKED ME TO TAKE HIS PICTURE, AS HE WANTED TO SEE HOW FUNNY HE LOOKED. IT WAS PRETTY GRIM, AND I DIDN'T FOCUS WELL.' Lee Miller was the only woman correspondent at the siege of St Malo: *above,* at a US tent hospital in northern France; *right,* with GIs; *below,* German prisoners, under close guard, used as litter bearers; *opposite,* waves of Allied bombers, at fifteen-minute intervals, attack the citadel of St Malo, 1944

PUSHING INTO GERMANY: *1,* burned bones of starved prisoners. *2,* homeless German women cook in the ruins, 1945. *3,* German civilians wait to cross the Main at Frankfurt by a little ferry boat. *4,* pilloried Nazi labelled as a food thief. *5,* Lee Miller luxuriates in the bath in Hitler's Munich apartment. *6,* a GI, relaxing on Hitler's bed, guards telephone connections

A CAMERA IN THE DESERT: Cecil Beaton, official war photographer, helps piece together an impression of the battlefield through freak shapes, curious perspectives, and fighting men. *Opposite above, below left, and below right,* macabre and beautiful abstractions of destruction in the Western Desert: skeleton that was an Italian plane; patchwork that was Tobruk's fire station roof; a pattern that was a German tank at Sidi Rezegh; 1942. *Left,* an officer of the British Eighth Army fights his way through a desert sandstorm to his tent, camouflaged with fishnet, 1943. *Top,* the white ensign is hoisted over Tobruk, 1943. *Above,* Beaton sightseeing near Cairo, 1942

ENTERTAINING THE TROOPS: _Below,_ Fred Astaire in khaki, dancing for the boys. _Right,_ night bivouac, Camp Croft: Private Zero Mostel amusing his company, 1943. _Far right,_ Marlene Dietrich making a besequinned entrance from a tent dressing-room somewhere in Italy, 1944. She was a regular USO performer both at stations at home and abroad. _Vogue_ listed how she made up her 55 lb baggage allowance for Destinations Unknown: two long sequinned gowns, a strapless brocade dress, transparent Vinylite slippers, grey flannel men's pants, silk-lined cashmere sweater by Mainbocher, tropical uniforms, and lingerie. She also took three months' worth of cosmetics, labelled in huge nailpolish letters (for dressing by torchlight) and a soap she had specially made to lather in practically no water, for her hair

'THEY, THE CHILDREN – THE REAL EXPENDABLES': *Opposite, above,* US Marines and Japanese babies suffer together on Okinawa, 1945. INTERNATIONAL NEWS. *Opposite, below,* a refugee peasant carries her child along the roads of northern France during the retreat of the shattered Ninth Army, 1940. The Panzer divisions are only half an hour behind. THERESE BONNEY. *Left,* strange bedfellows: leathernecks and a native boy share a foxhole on Okinawa, 1945. SGT WILLIAM McBRIDE, USMCR. *Above,* 'now there's not a child with legs as sturdy nor shoes as stout as these.' Refugee child, 1942. THERESE BONNEY

WAR AT BOTH ENDS OF THE EARTH: *Above,* pitted and broken by gunfire, the University of the Philippines in Manila is reduced to a rococo ruin, 1945. 'Now the city and the slums are one,' wrote *Vogue's* Pacific correspondent, Mary Jean Kempner, after fierce fighting drove the Japanese from the city and forced their surrender. 'Manila devastated by war, lies prostrate, filthy, stinking.' US SIGNAL CORPS. *Right,* French peasants put flowers on a dead American soldier, killed in front of their house, 1945. This photograph accompanied an article in American *Vogue* by Marya Mannes entitled 'Question to American women: who is doing your part in the war?' At the time America was looking for 14,000 nurses and 50,000 nurses' aides. 'Our guest this evening is a dead American soldier. He is sprawled out stiffened with mud, but he is listening. He may possibly be the husband of one of you here, or a son – I don't know because his identification tag is covered with a dark stain. But he will be especially interested in your answers, because it will depend partly on them whether he died betrayed, or because one of you wasn't there to stop his blood from running out.' US SIGNAL CORPS

ON BOTH SIDES, CIVILISATION LIES IN RUINS. *Right,* end of a myth: Hitler's Eagle's Nest at Berchtesgaden flames to destruction, 1945. LEE MILLER. *Top,* Curzon Street framed by bombed London streets, 1945. Drawn by Feliks Topolski, *Vogue* contributor and official war artist. *Above left,* the Queen stands beside the King in the bombed wreckage of the Palace, 1941. *Above right,* the interior of St Stephen's Cathedral, Vienna, shattered by Red Army shellfire, stands supported by scaffolding, 1945. LEE MILLER

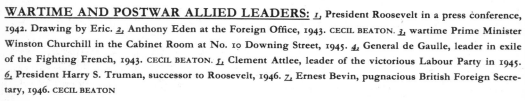

WARTIME AND POSTWAR ALLIED LEADERS: *1,* President Roosevelt in a press conference, 1942. Drawing by Eric. *2,* Anthony Eden at the Foreign Office, 1943. CECIL BEATON. *3,* wartime Prime Minister Winston Churchill in the Cabinet Room at No. 10 Downing Street, 1945. *4,* General de Gaulle, leader in exile of the Fighting French, 1943. CECIL BEATON. *5,* Clement Attlee, leader of the victorious Labour Party in 1945. *6,* President Harry S. Truman, successor to Roosevelt, 1946. *7,* Ernest Bevin, pugnacious British Foreign Secretary, 1946. CECIL BEATON

5

6

7

The Liberation of Paris

BY LEE MILLER

Paris had gone mad . . . The avenues were crowded with flags and filled with screaming, cheering people. Girls, bicycles, kisses and wine and around the corner sniping, a bursting tank. The bullet holes in the windows were like jewels, the barbed wire in the boulevards, a new decoration. The Parisians had made a fantastic game of their week of war . . . the stakes were life and death, but in their long-awaited battle they attacked with gaiety, irresponsibility and flowers in their hair.

Boys who had grown up under the occupation gained rifles and manhood in one gesture . . . they fought at the barricades, swarmed over roof tops and sniped snipers . . . Girls in flippant clothes carried ammunition, food and messages. The much-ridiculed French telephone system continued to function: Jean-Pierre could ask Philippe to drop his grenades into a courtyard nest of *krauts*.

I arrived exhausted by my share of millions of handshakes – handshakes for the *femme soldat*. The next day, Paris started cleaning up after the world's most gigantic party. Shops rolled up their shutters and trimmed their windows with merchandise which they had hoarded in the years of Occupation. The great dress-houses opened their doors and a few cafés tentatively put out chairs – to be immediately swamped and overflowed.

Everywhere in the streets were the dazzling girls, cycling, crawling up tank turrets. Their silhouette was very queer and fascinating to me after utility and austerity England. Full floating skirts, tiny waist-lines. They were top-heavy with built-up pompadour-front hair-dos and waving tresses; weighted to the ground with clumsy, fancy thick-soled wedge shoes.

They deliberately organised this style of dressing as a taunt to the Huns, whose women, dressed in grey uniforms, were known as the *Souris Gris*. If the Germans wore cropped hair, the French grew theirs long. If three yards of material were specified for a dress, they found fifteen for a skirt alone. Saving material and labour meant help to the Germans – and it was their duty to waste instead of to save.

La Ville Lumière is no more . . . not because it is black-out but because there is literally no light: there has not been enough coal to make electricity for weeks. The *métro* has closed down branch by branch, the buses have stopped and current is supplied for twenty minutes in twenty-four hours. Candles are a fabulous treasure.

There is one hairdresser in all Paris who can dry your hair: Gervais. He has rigged his dryers to stove pipes which pass through a furnace heated by rubble. The air is sent by fans turned by relay teams of boys riding a stationary tandem bicycle in the basement. They cover 320 kilometres a day and dry 160 heads . . .

I called on Michel de Brunhoff, editor of former Paris *Vogue*. He was *exalté* and voluble about the liberation in spite of the tragedy of his son's execution . . . Bébé Bérard and Boris Kochno had spent the battle of Paris on their balcony loading guns for six French resistance boys who were shooting up the snipers.

Picasso and I fell into each other's arms and between laughter and tears we exchanged news about friends and their work, incoherently, and looked at new pictures which were dated on all the Battle of Paris days . . .

1, Michel de Brunhoff, editor of the suspended Paris *Vogue,* with Jean Pagès, a former *Vogue* artist. A few days before the Liberation, de Brunhoff's son was executed by the Gestapo. *2,* barbed wire rings the Place de la Concorde, 1944. LEE MILLER. *3,* despite the Liberation, there is still no transport except bicycles. Outfit for cycling: white rayon smocked with blue; apron over-skirt neatly meets behind. *4,* after the Battle of Paris, Lee Miller visits her old friend Picasso in his studio.

VOGUE CELEBRATES VICTORY: _1,_ London victory fantasy, drawn by Carel Weight, 1945. _2,_ V-E day in New York, 1945. _3,_ Churchill's famous Victory sign, 1945. _4,_ British, American, and Russian forces join for victory at Torgau in Germany, 1945. LEE MILLER. _Opposite,_ Sketch by Eric celebrating V-J day and the end of America's war, 1945

'LIBERATION: Vision of a day of perfect joy', by Raoul Dufy, 1944

Faces in Vogue

'Last year debutantes curtsied to Royalty in fairy story surroundings,' wrote *Vogue* in 1940. 'This year they will not curtsey to Royalty at all: unless it be during the inspection of a branch of National Service . . . Last year they lunched in each other's houses, dressed to the teeth for Ranelagh or Roehampton. This year they have staggered snack-bar lunches, dressed simply and suitably for canteen work or Red Cross classes . . . Last year women were running households. This year they are running canteens, voluntary organisations, service units – and taking orders as well as giving them.'

The war brought about nothing less than a social revolution in Britain. There was no place in beleaguered times for extravagant behaviour and exhibitionism. Mothers clubbed together to give balls in hotels as no-one had the space or the money for massive entertaining. Idle weekending in country houseparties was over, as was the formal Court presentation of debutantes, wearing their three white ostrich feathers and suffering agonies of nervousness as they backed away. (More democratic royal garden parties later took its place.) After the war, the season was never more than a weak shadow of its former self. 'At the moment, the snobbishness of the London season is at a low ebb,' wrote *Vogue* in 1948, 'because our society is in a state of flux and transition. People are not quite sure what or whom they should be snobbish about. Ancient names and high-sounding titles do not impress as they used to do; even wealth is no longer final master of the scene, because, in an age dominated by Marxist ideas, people feel a little shy of ownership.'

Royalty remained beloved and exemplary figureheads. During the war, the King and Queen bolstered the morale of the country, visiting bombed areas and giving encouragement to the bereft and homeless. When Buckingham Palace was bombed, the Queen was reputed to have said, 'At last I can look the East End in the face.' Princess Elizabeth overcame parental opposition and joined the ATS. Queen Mary was evacuated to Badminton House as the guest of the Duke of Beaufort. She ate Woolton pie like her subjects and gave lifts in her Daimler to amazed hitch-hiking servicemen. After the war, the wedding of Princess Elizabeth and Lieutenant Philip Mountbatten in 1947 gave the still-austerity-bound country a much-needed lift.

Elizabeth's younger sister Margaret was cast in a more independent, frivolous mould. The 'Princess Margaret set', including Sharman Douglas, daughter of the American ambassador, drank pink champagne and danced till dawn in nightclubs. After the war, Margaret took a trip on her own to France and Italy, and her romance with commoner Group Captain Peter Townsend had people agog.

The women who made news in gossip columns tended to be American heiresses or actresses. Barbara Hutton divorced the Count Haugwitz-Reventlow and married Cary Grant amid much publicity. Actress Rita Hayworth married Aly Khan. The glamorous ceremony – the swimming pool was filled with white wine and flowers – was officiated over by a French Communist mayor. But in general, the war found work for idle hands, and the ladies who appeared on *Vogue*'s pages were frequently shown doing voluntary work or pursuing careers of their own. Of necessity, the war liberated women to earn their own living and develop their talents.

Opposite, Lady Louis Mountbatten, painted by Salvador Dali, 1940. *Above*, Queen Elizabeth with Princess Elizabeth and Princess Margaret, 1944. CECIL BEATON

Journalism was a popular and respectable career. The staff of Condé Nast included many well-born ladies; Lady Stanley of Alderley was a *Vogue* fashion editor, Clarissa Churchill – who later married Anthony Eden – the magazine's feature editor, and Loelia, Duchess of Westminster, worked as a contributing editor of *House & Garden*. Not all were as spirited and independent as Sarah Churchill, the Prime Minister's daughter, who much against the desires of her parents became a success on the stage.

Edwina Mountbatten came into her own in the Forties. One of the giddiest Bright Young Things in the Twenties, she headed the St John Ambulance during the war. Afterwards, she accompanied her husband Lord Louis, the last Viceroy, to India, where as a friend of both Nehru and Jinnah she played a prominent part in India's transition to independence and was awarded the GBE.

Top, drawing of the wedding of Princess Elizabeth and Lieutenant Philip Mountbatten in Westminster Abbey, by _Vogue_ artist Feliks Topolski, 1947. _Above,_ cover of _Vogue's_ royal wedding issue, December 1947. ERIC. _Left,_ their Royal Highnesses the bride and bridegroom leaving in their coach after the wedding. _Opposite,_ the Princess's wedding dress: ivory satin delicately starred with pearl and crystal roses, wheat, and orange blossom

Top left, Mrs Alec Hambro, formerly Baba Beaton, 1949. CECIL BEATON. *Top right,* Loelia, Duchess of Westminster, contributing editor of *House & Garden,* 1948. CECIL BEATON. *Above left,* the Countess of Caernarvon, otherwise the dancer Tilly Losch, 1946. CECIL BEATON. *Above right,* Mrs Charles Sweeny, 1946. As Margaret Whigham she was Deb of the Year; later she became the Duchess of Argyll. *Opposite,* Countess Haugwitz-Reventlow, the Woolworth heiress Barbara Hutton, 1940. HORST

Opposite, 17-year-old Mrs Pasquale de Cicco, formerly Gloria Vanderbilt, 1942. HORST. *Above,* 20-year-old Brenda Frazier, most famous American debutante of the Thirties, now in war relief work, 1941. RAWLINGS. *Top right,* couturier's daughter Gogo Schiaparelli on her marriage to Robert Berenson, son of Bernard Berenson, 1941. HORST. *Centre,* Miss Jacqueline Bouvier with other debutantes at a Newport ball, 1947. *Right,* Leslie Nast, daughter of *Vogue's* founder Condé Nast, marries Lord St Just, 1949. CECIL BEATON

Top left, Lord and Lady Vansittart, 'she as beautiful as he is ruthless in his policy to suppress the Hun', 1944. *Top right,* the Duke and Duchess of Norfolk; he was Parliamentary Secretary to the Ministry of Agriculture, she worked in a shipyard, 1944. *Above left,* Mrs Lewis W. Douglas, wife of the American Ambassador to Britain, and her daughter Sharman, Vassar student and leading light in the 'Princess Margaret set', 1947. HORST. *Above right,* Leopold Stennett Amery, Secretary of State for India and Burma, and his wife, 1944. CECIL BEATON. *Opposite,* Lady Diana Cooper in the gardens at Chantilly when her husband was Ambassador to France, 1946

Top left, Eve Curie, journalist daughter of scientist Marie, 1940. HORST. *Top right*, playwright, journalist, and war correspondent Clare Booth Luce, 1940. HORST. *Above left*, Pamela Churchill, wife of Randolph and mother of Winston, 1946. RAWLINGS.

Above right, actress Sarah Churchill, daughter of the Prime Minister and wife of Vic Oliver, 1941. CECIL BEATON. *Opposite*, Clarissa Churchill, niece of the Prime Minister and *Vogue's* feature editor; later she became Mrs Anthony Eden, 1949. CECIL BEATON

Ballet Crazy

Ballet performances were curtailed for much of the war. Afterwards, audiences went mad for dancing. 'London is still ecstatically ballet-drunk,' wrote *Vogue* in 1947. That March there were four ballet companies dancing in London and as many ballet periodicals on the book stalls.

Covent Garden, which for much of the war had been used as a *palais de danse* for the forces, reopened with the Sadlers Wells in residence. The company's principal choreographer Frederick Ashton, who had spent the war in the RAF – with occasional leave to work on ballets – produced some fresh and enchanting work, including *Cinderella,* the first full-length classical ballet by an English choreographer. Danced to music by Prokofiev, it starred the witty actor-dancer Robert Helpmann and Ashton himself *en grande tenue* as the Ugly Sisters. *Vogue* described them as 'brilliantly funny and subtly malevolent'. In 1946 Ashton collaborated with his friends Cecil Beaton and Lord Berners on *Les Sirènes*, a brittle little Edwardian joke. Set in Trouville in the 1900s, it had the diamond huntress Margot Fonteyn, swathed in motoring veils, chugging on stage in a period automobile, while Ashton himself as an oriental potentate floated down from the ceiling in a huge gas balloon. Beaton's sets had a Brighton Pavilion look.

Margot Fonteyn, the company's prima ballerina, was perfection to watch in *Giselle* and *Swan Lake,* although the vivacious young Moira Shearer was also tipped for stardom, and they alternated roles in many ballets. Shearer played in the ballet film *The Red Shoes* with Massine, 'perhaps the most pathetic, gentlest, wittiest, gayest, greatest of them all'. *Vogue*'s reviewer Siriol Hugh Jones, attending the shooting, felt she was watching the evolution of 'an entirely new art, choreo-photography'.

The Sadlers Wells made a triumphant tour of America in 1949. Five of the twelve ballets they performed were English and contemporary: *Façade, Job, Checkmate, The Rake's Progress,* and *Miracle in the Gorbals,* the first 'working-class' ballet.

But the flow was not only one way. Three years earlier, the American Ballet Theatre had brought its dramatic and high-spirited 'American-style' ballets to Covent Garden. Their great hit was *Fancy Free*, a graceful roughhouse, choreographed with witty, soft-shoe routines by the prolific twenty-seven-year-old Jerome Robbins to music by Leonard Bernstein. (The musical comedy *Look Ma, I'm Dancing* was based on Robbins' idea about a ballet troupe on tour.) Anthony Tudor, previously an English accountant, danced with the Ballet Theatre, and the 'bone-beautiful' Alicia Markova partnered Anton Dolin in the company's new version of *Firebird*, against a colour-swirling set by Chagall. Dolin also danced with Baranova, back from making movies in Hollywood ('Just another ballerina gone west,' wrote *Vogue* when she went), in *Bluebeard*, staged by Fokine, with comic-horror sets by Vertès.

America also boasted two other major ballet companies, as well as a spate of minor ones. The Ballets Russes, with its part-Indian ballerina Rosella Hightower, was back after five years spent touring Latin America during the war. The Ballets Russes de Monte Carlo, proud of its star Alexandra Danilova, danced vigorous classics and American ballets, including one with Gershwin music, characters from the cartoons in the *New Yorker*, and a central figure who was a nationally known gossip columnist. Then there was also the Ballet Society, formed by Lincoln Kirsten and Balan-

Above, the ballroom scene from *Apparitions* with Margot Fonteyn and Robert Helpmann, 1949. CECIL BEATON. *Opposite,* Alicia Markova and Anton Dolin take their gala bow after *Giselle,* 1944. ERIC

chine, which gave small, highly professional performances of avant-garde works like Colette's *L'Enfant et les Sortilèges*, set to music by Ravel.

The rising star of French ballet was Roland Petit – 'a vivid and decorative personality, an original choreographer' – who still helped his father serve in his small café in the market *quartier* of Paris and slept in a little room at the back of the bar. He danced for the Ballets des Champs Elysées, Boris Kochno's troupe, along with the astonishing twelve-year-old Ethery Pagava and Leslie Caron, young and unforgettable as the Sphinx to Jean Babilée's Oedipus in *La Rencontre*. The Champs Elysées was known less for its disciplined dance than its lively and imaginative repertoire. Jean Cocteau's *Le Jeune Homme et la Mort* was a piece about a fatal love which had kickings, spittings, and Jean Babilée dancing on the edge of a table and hanging himself on stage. It was rehearsed to jazz tunes and then danced at the same speed to Bach. 'Unfortunately the theme is too morbid and meaningless, the music too beautiful, for the effect to be other than irritating,' wrote *Vogue*'s Clarissa Churchill.

In 1948, Petit formed his own company, the Ballet de Paris. In his ballet *Carmen* he danced a doomed Don José to his discovery, Zizi Jeanmaire, who made a dazzling little Bal-Tabarin Carmen with a wicked glitter and an 'existentialist' haircut. *Vogue* called her 'the most exciting young ballerina in years'.

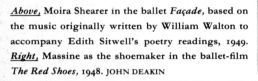

Above, Moira Shearer in the ballet _Façade,_ based on the music originally written by William Walton to accompany Edith Sitwell's poetry readings, 1949. _Right,_ Massine as the shoemaker in the ballet-film _The Red Shoes,_ 1948. JOHN DEAKIN

Left, Alexandra Danilova dancing with Frederick Franklin at Covent Garden, 1949. PENN. _Above, The Rake's Progress,_ choreographed by Ninette de Valois and designed by Rex Whistler after Hogarth's 18th-century paintings, 1949. _Opposite,_ Robert Helpmann and Frederick Ashton as the Ugly Sisters in Ashton's _Cinderella,_ designed by Malclès and danced to Prokofiev's music at Covent Garden, 1949

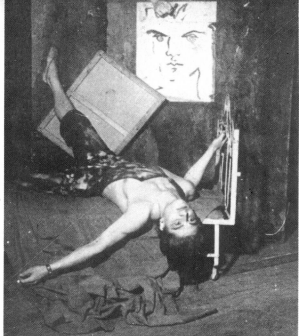

Top left, André Eglevsky of the Grand Ballet de Monte Carlo, 1949. 'He looks like a combination of a fawn and a Mack truck.' PENN. *Top centre,* Jean Babilée as the moribund young man in his garret in the Cocteau ballet, *Le Jeune Homme et la Mort,* 1946. *Top,* Roland Petit dancing in a costume by Christian Dior, 1948. GILLES. *Left,* choreographer Jerome Robbins, lying on the floor surrounded by ten dancers from six of his ballets danced in the 1948 New York season. GJON MILI. *Above,* crop-haired Renée Jeanmaire (Zizi) in the role of Carmen, created for her by Roland Petit, 1949. *Opposite,* the American Ballet Theatre's *Bluebeard,* staged by Fokine, with comic-horror sets and costumes by Vertès. It starred Anton Dolin as Bluebeard and Baranova as the Sixth Wife, 1942

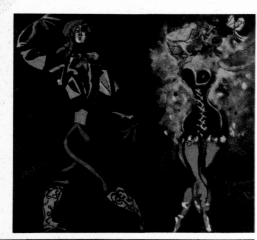

Top, costume designs for _Carmen_ by Clavé, 1949. _Above_, Bérard's sketches for the Kochno ballet _La Rencontre_, 1949. _Right_, _Fancy Free_, designed and danced by Jerome Robbins (left) with John Kriza and Harold Lang, 1944. ERIC. _Below_, costumes by Keogh for Boris Kochno's _Till Eulenspiegel_ with Jean Babilée, 1949. _Below right_, design by Forains for _Les Amours de Jupiter_, 1946. _Opposite_, design by Beaurepaire for _Concert de Danses_, starring Solange Schwartz, 1946

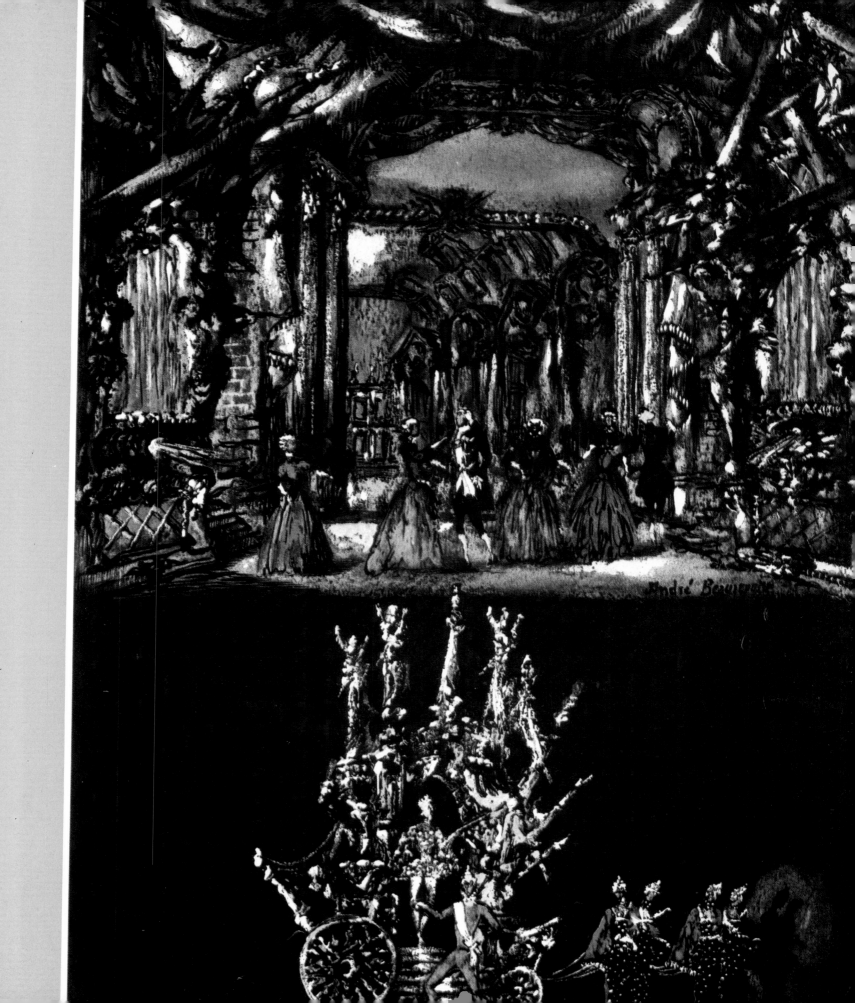

Broadway at theatre-time, 1948. BLUMENFELD

Treading the Boards

During the war, people flocked to the theatre for a welcome and much-needed relaxation from day-to-day concerns. 'Today any successful play stands a chance of running for the duration, until desperation, or large scale air-raids, send the people back to their lairs, until the leading lady becomes too old for her own part, or dies from a lack of essential fats and juices,' wrote Cecil Beaton. There was a slight hiccup at the outset, when theatres opened and closed rather unpredictably, but the show went on. By 1943 there were 37 theatres open in London and 31 on Broadway. London audiences adapted to a 5 o'clock curtain up, and to unheated theatres. Jean Anouilh, writing in *Vogue*, told of ski clothes being *de rigueur* in Parisian theatres, and of one old gentleman in a balaclava helmet who fainted from cold 'quite properly, during the interval' at one performance.

Some of the theatre's best exponents, among them Ralph Richardson, Raymond Massey, Michael Redgrave, John Mills and Alec Guinness, were away in uniform. The Old Vic was bombed and became hydra-headed, its companies scattering over the country. Noel Coward also took his company on tour and delighted provincial audiences with *Blithe Spirit*, *This Happy Breed*, and *Present Laughter*.

Wartime theatrical fare tended to be safe, nostalgic and fun. No-one except the critics was interested in words like 'proletarian' and 'social significance'. 'Out of a list of 19 non-musical shows, seven are revivals and seven are American, which points out that only five are English or original,' noted Beaton in 1943. Londoners got their share of English drawing-room comedies like *Lady Windermere's Fan*, Pinero's *Dandy Dick*, and *The Merry Widow*. But writers like Shaw and Chekhov were also successful commercial propositions – the success of *The Doctor's Dilemma* was not only due to the beauty of Vivien Leigh. After the war, Raymond Massey and Gertrude Lawrence thoroughly enjoyed themselves in a 1946 production of *Pygmalion*, 'partly because they can move about in Shaw's slashing characters'. A revival of *Cyrano de Bergerac*, with Ralph Richardson in London and José Ferrer in New York, was a smash success.

People adored *Life with Father*, an affectionately ironic play about the family of Clarence Day, performed in London by Leslie Banks. They lapped up *Harvey*, the story of a drunk and his six-foot one-and-a-half-inch invisible white rabbit – 'sheer heaven, common sense transmuted into wisdom'. Even murder was funny when performed by two old ladies in *Arsenic and Old Lace*. George S. Kaufman and Moss Hart sadistically pickled their friend Alexander Woollcott for all time in *The Man Who Came To Dinner*, helped out by tinkling tunes from Cole Porter.

On Broadway, America's glittering theatrical couple Alfred Lunt and Lynn Fontanne kept audiences enraptured, acting to the hilt in a succession of romps that culminated in *I Know My Love*, a tender duet to their fifty years of marriage.

Noel Coward kept spirits up – literally – with his ingenious *Blithe Spirit*, with Margaret Rutherford as the clairvoyant and Kay Hammond as the ethereal ghost. It became the longest-running play on the London stage and the outstanding wartime success, comparable with *Chu Chin Chow* and *The Man Who Stayed at Home* in the previous war.

The darlings of the British theatre were Laurence Olivier and his wife Vivien Leigh. Olivier's Broadway production of *Romeo and Juliet* – 'the true-life love story of Scarlett O'Hara and Rebecca's Max de Winter' – in 1940 received tepid press notices but nonetheless thrilled their fans. Olivier's towering genius and energy led him from triumph to triumph and to a knighthood in 1947. His *Richard III* made theatrical history. 'He imbued the arch-villain of tradition with a silky, sinister sort of sex appeal,' wrote *Vogue*'s Lesley Blanch. 'Slithy is the right word, I think.' His most ambitious undertaking, his 1946 production of *King Lear* at the Old Vic, was sold out months in advance. His rendering of the part, traditionally regarded as unactable, was considered as one of the peaks of a glittering career.

After the war, Olivier took the Old Vic on tour to New York, and later to Australia and New Zealand, acting with Ralph Richardson in *Henry IV* and with Vivien Leigh in *School for Scandal*. In the latter he played Sir Peter Teazle with a dropping chin and querulous eye, while his wife made an adorable Lady Teazle in Romney-style black elegance designed by Cecil Beaton. Miss Leigh showed her range in parts as different as Anouilh's tragic modern-dress *Antigone* and Sabina in Thornton Wilder's imaginative history of humanity, *The Skin of Our Teeth* – 'that sluttish, film-conscious, mouse-minded, heroic, wildly feminine little inspiration, the other woman in person.' *Vogue* called it her best part. In America, Sabina was acted with abandon by Tallulah Bankhead.

Another prolific English theatrical figure was John Gielgud. The nephew of Ellen Terry, he was renowned for the 'Terry voice', and was, like Olivier, producer, actor, and director. Among his successful roles was that of Raskolnikov in Rodney Ackland's adaptation of *Crime and Punishment*, which he played with a terrible cumulative tension. Peter Ustinov as the detective and Dame Edith Evans as the consumptive wife of the drunken neighbour contributed to a credible and moving performance. Ustinov, frequently described by the British press as 'our very own Orson Welles', also had a number of his own plays performed over the decade, including *House of Regrets* and *Paris Not so Gay*.

Shakespeare, reassuringly traditional in troubled times, was eagerly revived on both sides of the Atlantic. British audiences saw Michael Redgrave as Macbeth, Alec Guinness as Richard II and the Fool in Olivier's *King Lear*, and Trevor Howard in *The Taming of the Shrew*. The young Paul Scofield at Stratford immersed himself in the Shakespearean canon, playing Hamlet, Troilus, Mercutio, Lucio in *Measure for Measure*, and Armado in *Love's Labour's Lost*, a lovely Watteau-like *fête galante* produced by the twenty-two-year-old Peter Brook. 'If any proof were needed that Peter Brook is one of our most imaginative and courageous young producers, we have it in this play,' wrote *Vogue*. 'His work impresses one by a firm and unwavering judgement that is rare in so young a man.'

On Broadway, Helen Hayes and Maurice Evans turned *Twelfth Night* into a carnival, and Paul Robeson with his tolling voice made a magnificent Othello. José Ferrer played Iago like a matador, on the tip of his toes, manipulating the Moor and the virginally white Uta Hagen with a virtuoso's delight in his technique.

The war inevitably inspired a number of plays. Cecil Beaton produced a pantomime for the troops, with scenery by Augustus John and Rex Whistler, and most of Debrett strutting the boards. There was Noel Coward's *This Happy Breed* – 'Cavalcade seen

through the wrong end of opera glasses: the perspective has dimmed the national glamour and drama but the spirit remains.' Maxwell Anderson's *The Eve of St Mark* was a touching and sensitive piece about new boys in the army, 'steeled with inspiration, soaked in tears, and broken with laughter'. Montgomery Clift gave an extraordinary performance as the wounded soldier in Lillian Hellman's tense play *The Searching Wind*, with its line about Mussolini's entrance into Rome in 1922: 'Like an operation – just a few minutes more and the patient will be an invalid for life.'

In Britain, Terence Rattigan's *Flare Path*, a serious comedy about the RAF, in which the author was himself serving, became the unofficial dramatic symbol of the war. Despite criticism that it was bad for morale, it ran endlessly, and was produced simultaneously in Moscow and New York.

The end of the war unleashed a spate of significant plays. *The Cocktail Party* by Nobel Prize winner T.S. Eliot had its première in 1949 at the recently inaugurated Edinburgh Festival. In 1946 Cocteau, by then sixty, had five simultaneous successes: a ballet, a film, a book, and two plays – *Les Parents Terribles* and his hymn to death, *The Eagle Has Two Heads*. The English version of this thunderous Gothic extravaganza starred statuesque Eileen Herlie.

Another Frenchman, Jean-Paul Sartre, stunned audiences with his brilliant *Huis Clos*, an existentialist merry-go-round for three newly dead murderers: a coward, a lesbian, and a man-hunter. Shut in a hideous Second-Empire hotel room, they begin to make their own hell in a vicious circle from which there is no exit.

There was also *Caligula*, a play by the young existentialist thinker Albert Camus, with Gérard Philippe in the lead, and a posthumous play by Giraudoux, entitled *The Madwoman of Chaillot*. A life-affirming fantasy on the future of the human race, it was a terrific success in Paris, London, and New York. Its director, the famous Girauducian actor Louis Jouvet, had left France during the war and gone to South America to avoid the Gestapo. Set designer Christian Bérard became a ragpicker like one of the characters when he asked Parisians to donate authentic period clothing, from which he designed the costumes and miraculously imaginative sets.

The American Arthur Miller – 'not yet a famous writer' – was the author of two successful plays: *All My Sons*, and his masterpiece *Death of a Salesman*. The salesman Willie Loman and his family are so caught in the dream of success that they can't get back to fact. In complete contrast – although it was also about a travelling salesman – was Eugene O'Neill's *The Ice Man Cometh*. The theme of this arduous five-hour drama stressed the importance of preserving one's illusions.

Playwright Tennessee Williams produced two stunning plays. Laurette Taylor was dubbed the star of the year in 1945 for her role as a Southern belle with memories in *The Glass Menagerie*. Four years later, a blonde Vivien Leigh in London, and Arletty in France, played Blanche in *A Streetcar Named Desire*. Twenty-three-year-old Marlon Brando as the inarticulate Stanley Kowalski (in the New York production) was the embodiment of primitive, erupting passion in a claustrophobic Southern summer.

1. **Martita Hunt as Miss Haversham and Valerie Hobson as Estella in *Great Expectations,* 1946.** CECIL BEATON. *2.* **Nora Swinburne as Natalia in *A Month in the Country*, 1943.** CECIL BEATON. *3.* **Judy Campbell, dressed by Molyneux, playing the dusky seductress in *Present Laughter* with Noel Coward's touring company, 1942.** CECIL BEATON. *4.* **Vivien Leigh, blonde for her part as Blanche in *A Streetcar named Desire*, 1949.** *5.* **Isabel Jeans in *Lady Windermere's Fan*, 1946.** CECIL BEATON. *6.* **the suburban wedding group from Noel Coward's *This Happy Breed*, 1942.** CECIL BEATON

1

1, Paul Scofield as Hamlet at Stratford, 1948. JOHN DEAKIN. **2,** Laurence Olivier as Richard III, drawn by Topolski, 1948. **3,** John Gielgud in *Crime and Punishment,* sketched by Bouché, 1946. **4,** Peter Brook, 21-year-old producer of *Love's Labour's Lost,* 1946. COFFIN. **5,** Peter Ustinov, actor, producer and director, 1947. COFFIN. **6,** Robert Morley, actor and playwright, 1948. **7,** Peggy Ashcroft as Titania, 1945. **8,** Patricia Burke and Trevor Howard in *The Taming of the Shrew,* 1947. COFFIN. **9,** Joyce Redman and Rex Harrison in Maxwell Anderson's *Anne of the Thousand Days,* 1949

1, Tallulah Bankhead as Miss Atlantic City in Thornton Wilder's *The Skin of our Teeth,* 1943. *2,* 21-year-old Marlon Brando, 'a wilful theatrical talent', 1946. CECIL BEATON. *3,* Burgess Meredith as Christy in *The Playboy of the Western World,* 1946. *4,* actor Clifton Webb, 1949. *5,* Alfred Lunt and Lynn Fontanne, stars of *O Mistress Mine,* 1946. CECIL BEATON. *6,* Katharine Cornell in Jean Anouilh's *Antigone,* 1946. *7,* Arthur Miller's harrowing *Death of a Salesman,* starring Lee J. Cobb, Mildred Dunnock, and Arthur Kennedy on a set designed by Jo Mielziner, 1949. CECIL BEATON

1

_1._ Montgomery Clift as the wounded corporal in Lillian Hellman's controversial play _The Searching Wind_, 1944. RAWLINGS. _2._ John Garfield and Nancy Kelly in Clifford Odet's murder melodrama _The Big Knife_, 1949. _3._ Margaret Sullavan and Elliot Nugent in _The Voice of the Turtle_, 1943. _4._ Laurette Taylor in _The Glass Menagerie_, 1945. _5._ Shirley Booth, Sam Wanamaker, and Madeleine Carroll, stars of _Goodbye My Fancy_, 1949. _6._ Paul Robeson as a tortured Othello, 1943. _7._ Judith Anderson giving a 'nerve-wrought' performance as Medea, 1947

1, Charles Boyer in a Broadway production of Jean-Paul Sartre's *Les Mains Sales,* 1949. 2, Arletty, 1949. She played Blanche in the Parisian version of *A Streetcar named Desire*. 3, Jean-Louis Barrault, actor and all-round man of the French theatre, 1949. PENN. 4, Louis Jouvet as Molière's Don Juan, 1948. COFFIN. 5, Marguerite Moréno as the eponymous heroine in Giraudoux's *La Folle de Chaillot,* directed by Louis Jouvet, 1946

Jean-Paul Sartre's *No Exit (Huis Clos)* on Broadway: Annabella, Ruth Ford, and Claude Dauphin played the three characters fighting in a dingy hotel room symbolic of hell, 1946

Funny Men and Women

'Wartime audiences love all that brassy, rip-the-roof-off quality which is a blend of traditional music-hall and imported vaudeville,' wrote *Vogue* in 1942. 'The blend is choice and very much to taste. Very tasty, in fact, if not very nice in the naicest sense. Vic Oliver, Tommy Trinder (Trinder's the name), Flanagan and Allen, Maxie Miller (feel it, lady!), Big-hearted Arthur Askey, and many more. And now, any minute, Carmen Miranda, the bauble-laden Brazilian bombshell, at present en route for ENSA concert platforms.'

English audiences also loved révues. In contrast with extravagant American musical comedies, this was a peculiarly English genre, up-to-the-minute, cheap and easy to put on, and suited to the English sense of humour. The Forties were particularly rich in a generation of funny women. Hermione Gingold was dubbed by *Vogue* 'the funniest woman in England' for her bold, bad tongue and unquenchable vitality. She appeared at the Ambassadors in writer Alan Melville's *Sweet and Low* (1943), which was followed by *Sweeter and Lower* (1944) and *Sweetest and Lowest* (1946), and was also writing a 'fantastic' autobiography entitled *The World is Square*. There was the other Hermione, Hermione Baddely, and the lanky Joyce Grenfell, a niece of Lady Astor, whose expression of simple gaiety and guileless sweet innocence overlaid an observation as precise and deadly as a new razor-blade. Famous for her 'How' broadcasts on the radio, she was also a great hit in *Tuppence Coloured* at the Lyric, Hammersmith, a witty revue for which Peter Brook contributed a Japanese ballet.

The singer Gracie Fields, 'who has a voice only a Lancashire man could love', had audiences holding their sides with her provincial protest at life in *Top Notches*. Two British women who were equally successful at home or in America were Gertrude Lawrence and the deadpan Beatrice Lillie, whose fascination was her sudden momentary plunge into lunatic clowning in the middle of a highly polished, sophisticated act.

There were funny men too: the Crazy Gang with Bud Flanagan, 'those angels of impossible logic'; George Robey, now eighty years old; the risqué Douglas Byng, who made a superbly elegant pantomime dame; and the Birmingham boy Sid Field, who immortalised the cockney 'spiv'. Newcomer Peter Ustinov, only nineteen years old, could be seen at the Players Club in 1940 doing his mad impersonations of Mme Liselotte Beethoven-Fincke, a suetty opera singer, and the lumpish, drooling Bishop of Limpopoland.

Noel Coward, pastmaster of the revue, produced *Sigh No More*. It starred Joyce Grenfell and made everyone feel frightfully in the know if they could identify his friends in the song 'Nina'. The great impresario C.B. Cochran brought out a string of shows – *Lights Up* (1940), *Big Top* (1942), a satire on Parliament called *Big Ben* (1946), and *Bless the Bride* (1947) – but none seemed to live up to his earlier successes.

America's answer to the revue was blue-eyed, India-rubber-faced Danny Kaye, who was adored on both sides of the Atlantic. Another favourite was Bop Hope, who spent much of his time entertaining the troops. Lesley Blanch was so exhilarated at meeting him that she didn't mind that someone stole her bag of kippers during the interview – no small loss in wartime.

Those high priests of comedy, the Marx Brothers, were still going strong, providing 'a sort of divine holiday from the rules of normal behaviour.'

Top, Hermione Baddeley conducts a terrible teaparty of old school friends in a Melville revue, 1948. COFFIN. *Above,* Douglas Byng, most superbly elegant of pantomime dames, 1948. *Opposite,* Beatrice Lillie clowns while Valentina fits her costume for *Seven Lively Arts,* 1944

Top and opposite right, two of the many faces of Joyce Grenfell, glittering
with schoolgirl enthusiasm, and emitting the wild notes of an Indian love-
call, 1947. JOHN DEAKIN. *Above and right,* Hermione Gingold, striking a
vigorous stance as a bemedalled Wren officer, and as Mother India, 'bony-
fingered, reticuled, and mouthing incomparable platitudes'. COFFIN.
Opposite left, Reginald Beckwith parodying a striptease at the Gate. 1940

Left, Bob Hope during a rehearsal at London's Odeon Theatre of his hugely successful USO Camp Show, 1944. LEE MILLER. _Above,_ zany comedian Michael Bentine, 1949. _Below left,_ 80-year-old George Robey, king of music-hall comics, 1948. _Below centre,_ Birmingham-bred comedian Sid Field, 1944. _Below right,_ Leslie Henson, star of _Bob's Your Uncle,_ 1948. _Opposite, Vogue_ 'symbolist' portrait of Danny Kaye. 'The brain suggests his cerebral wit; the feather stuck in it his jauntiness; the old overshoe his homely lack of pretension; the yoyo his wonderful timing; the violin and piccolo his shrill contrapuntal precision; the spring his steely bounce; the soda pop his easy sparkle; the gingerbread man and sand bucket his playfulness; the umbrella his curious elegance; the wig, the squash and the Chinese chicken, because they are blonde and bizarre.' 1946. PENN

Song and Dance

In 1943 the American musical reached new heights with *Oklahoma!* Composed by Richard Rodgers, with lyrics by his new collaborator Oscar Hammerstein II, it was the first musical in which music (folk-cowboy), plot, and ballet (by Agnes de Mille) meshed seamlessly. There was no chorus line, and no stopping for star performers. It was good, clean fun, exactly the values a wartime audience wanted. On Broadway it took $31,000 weekly; in London, *Vogue* called it 'a musical that cannot miss'.

Several prominent composers produced 'wartime' musicals. Irving Berlin wrote *This is the Army* ('Uncle Sam Presents'), which toured the United States and raised $5 million for Army Relief. *Winged Victory*, by Moss Hart, was acted by 300 US Air Force men. The Army commissioned the play. Hart was put on a bomber for seven weeks to visit air bases before writing the play about six boys, from their induction through their training to the South Pacific mission. *South Pacific*, with Mary Martin and dreamy songs like 'Some Enchanted Evening', also showed the Pacific war.

Cole Porter contributed to the war effort by writing the Marine Air Corps song, 'Sailors of the Air'. He also wrote *Panama Hattie*, which had Ethel Merman as a nightclub queen on the Panama Canal, and *Something for the Boys* (1943), in which she dressed up as a squaw. His big success of the decade was *Kiss Me Kate* (1948) based on *The Taming of the Shrew*.

Ethel Merman also sang Irving Berlin. Her brash and brassy voice made her the hit of *Annie Get Your Gun*, when she sang *Doin' What Comes Naturally*. Berlin's most famous song came from the 1942 musical *Holiday Inn*, with Bing Crosby: 'White Christmas'.

One of the greatest Broadway hits was *Carmen Jones*, a Negro musical starring Muriel Smith and produced by Billy Rose. 'A musical that socks the eye, but not always the ear,' was *Vogue*'s verdict. It took Bizet's music, but colloquial, new, witty lyrics by Oscar Hammerstein II. Another Negro star, Pearl Bailey, showed her gift for comedy in the musical *St Louis Woman*.

Carole Channing was making her name fast. She appeared in *Lend an Ear* in 1948 and a year later in *Gentlemen Prefer Blondes*. Anita Loos, author of the book and co-author of the musical, wrote an article in *Vogue* on 'The decline and fall of blondes', describing how the world had changed since the Twenties, when Lorelei Lee from Little Rock, Arkansas, was able to depend on gentlemen to buy her diamond bracelets. Postwar girls worked in factories and even chorus girls found they had to work hard.

There was also *Brigadoon*, with the agile young Scottish dancer James Jamieson (libretto by Alan Jay Lerner) and *Finian's Rainbow*. This daffy fairy tale complete with leprechaun, pot of gold, and a mythical Irish county called Glocca Morra was also a sharp satire on racial prejudice in the South. The Japanese-Irish star Sono Osato appeared in *On the Town*, a musical by the conductor Leonard Bernstein. *Look Ma, I'm Dancing*, about a ballet troupe on tour, featured Jerome Robbins' fantasy ballets.

British talents were unable to compete with this energetic outpouring: it was not the national forte, although Ivor Novello was now an institution. He produced *The Dancing Years*, which ran successfully, and *King's Rhapsody*, with Zena and Phyllis Dare, both hovering around sixty. 'Although Novello never flags as his years keep dancing on,' wrote *Vogue*, 'the British musical honestly seems to have died a living death.'

Scene from *Carmen Jones*, the souped-up Negro version of Bizet's *Carmen*. 1944. GJON MILI

1

1, Mary Martin, the 'cockeyed optimist' of *South Pacific,* 1949. BLUMENFELD. *2,* and *3,* the nightmare ballet and the 'surrey with the fringe on top' from *Oklahoma!,* 1943. *4,* Betty Hutton, star of *Panama Hattie,* 1940. *5,* Enzo Pinza, baritone star of *South Pacific,* 1949. BISSINGER. *6,* Pearl Bailey, 'prim and starchy and sexy and slo-ow voiced', 1946. RAWLINGS. *7,* Ella Logan and David Wayne in *Finian's Rainbow,* 1947. *8,* Ethel Merman in *Annie Get Your Gun,* 1946. RAWLINGS. *9,* seductive Brazilian singer Carmen Miranda, 1940. ANTON BRUEHL

1, Jerome Kern, prolific writer of musicals, including *Show Boat*, 1945. GJON MILI.
2, Carole Channing and Yvonne Adair in *Gentlemen Prefer Blondes*, 1949. BLUMENFELD.
3, Moss Hart with the script for his play *Winged Victory*, 1943. BALKIN. **4,** Kurt Weill,
composer of *Street Scene*, 1948. PENN. **5,** Irving Berlin watching a rehearsal of *This is
the Army*, 1942. TONI FRISSELL. **6,** Nanette Fabray, spirited star of *High Button Shoes*,
singing 'Papa, Won't You Dance with Me?', 1947. RUTLEDGE. **7,** Harold Lang and
Nancy Walker in *Look Ma, I'm Dancing*, 1948

Swooners and Crooners

The war brought forth an inevitable crop of sentimental and romantic songs. Vera Lynn immortalised the white cliffs of Dover; she had sung with Glenn Miller and his band before he went down in a light aeroplane over the Channel. Gracie Fields and the 'blonde warbler and gay charmer' Frances Day were also popular with the troops. 'Keep Smiling Through' gave everyone something to hum when the going got bad. Noel Coward's song 'Don't Let's be Beastly to the Germans, Let's Soften Their Defeat Again, Don't Let's be Beastly to the Hun', had the BBC dithering about whether to play it on the air. More directly, Frank Loesser wrote 'Praise the Lord and Pass the Ammunition', said to be based on the words of a US Army padre caught in the attack at Pearl Harbor. Both Allied and German soldiers had their own words to 'Lili Marlene'.

In France, Maurice Chevalier kept up morale. 'He walks onto the stage wearing the one and only straw hat, and everybody miraculously feels much better,' wrote *Vogue* on his visit to England in 1948. Tiny, red-haired Edith Piaf, La Môme, sang her wistful numbers in Parisian nightclubs and went on tour after the war to the US. 'She turns a song over in your heart, gently, as though it were a sleeping baby.'

From America came a controversial new generation of crooners. 'The swooner-crooner controversy has put editorial writers into a lovely sweat; for they see in the rise of Frank Sinatra, Perry Como and Dick Haymes all kinds of juvenile psychotic tendencies – just as though these writers hadn't ridden out the storms of Rudy Vallée's voice and come through to the peaceful harbours of middle age,' wrote *Vogue*. The biggest 'dream boy', Frank Sinatra, whose voice betokened high-school seduction, had his fans going into 'Sinatrances'. 'His low-toned, high-voltage performances are a series of breathless phrases, strung together with moans,' wrote *Vogue*. '"His effect on our girls is *immoral*," storm the opposition.' Bing Crosby said that Sinatra himself looked like a Sinatra fan – very young, very 'rave'. 'Me? I'm just a bedroom singer,' said Sinatra himself.

Newcomer Nat King Cole was also gaining popularity. And there were women crooners. Lena Horne sang 'The Man I Love' at the Savoy Plaza and Maxine Sullivan, with her cool lemonade voice, acted Titania in a dizzy stew of swing, *Swinging the Dream*. Louis Armstrong was Bottom.

Swing was changing. Trumpeter Dizzy Gillespie invented bebop. The West Indian calypso rhythm suddenly caught on: in 1945 *Rum and Coca-Cola* was on everyone's lips. Virgil Thomson, the enlightened critic of the *New York Herald Tribune*, reported in *Vogue* how American popular music, whether jazz, swing, or whatever, was loved and played all over the world. *Vogue* went to a jam session to listen to Billie Holliday, hot Chicago-style guitarist Eddie Condon, Duke Ellington on piano (by 1948 he had sold more than 20 million records), Bunk Johnson, Count Basie, Earl Hines, and Hot Lips Page. Just what *was* jazz, in all its forms, was still hard to define. 'Jazz is a sort of *tamed* catastrophe,' ventured Jean Cocteau. Paul Whiteman declared, 'I've been playing it for thirty years and I still don't know what it is.' 'Whatever it is – it has nothing to do with art,' sniffed Clive Bell. Or as Fats Waller informed an erudite young lady who wanted to know: 'If you've got to *ask*, you *ain't* got it.'

1. Bing Crosby, 1946. GJON MILI. *2, 3,* and *4,* 'new dream boys' Carl Brisson, Perry Como, Dick Haymes, 1946. HALSHAM. *5,* Frank Sinatra, 'the most significant figure of American mass entertainment since Valentino', 1944. *6.* Lena Horne, 1944. RAWLINGS. *7.* La Môme Piaf, 1947. GJON MILI. *8,* Larry Adler with his harmonica, 1946

1, Dizzy Gillespie, 'a founder and the most provocative practitioner of bebop', 1948. *2,* 'Duke Ellington enjoying himself at the piano', 1943. By 1948 he had sold more than 20 million records. *3,* Bunk Johnson, one of the pioneers of jazz, 1946. *4,* 'Hot Lips' Page, 1946. *5,* Earl 'Father' Hines, and behind him Count Basie, two great interpreters of boogie-woogie, 1946. *6,* blues singer Billie Holliday, 1946

1, scene at the barrack gates from *The True Story of Lili Marlene*, 1944. 2, Jack Oakie and Charlie Chaplin needling the totalitarians in *The Great Dictator*, 1940. 3, Penelope Dudley-Ward, star of *Demi Paradise*, photographed at Denham Studios, 1943. LEE MILLER. 4, Valerie Hobson of *Unpublished Story*, photographed in *Vogue's* burned-out studio, 1941. CECIL BEATON. 5, Leslie Howard with escaped Nazi officers in *Forty-Ninth Parallel*, 1941. 6, Clark Gable, US Air Force Gunnery Officer, in an army training film, 1943. 7, John Hodiak in Hitchcock's *Lifeboat*, 1944

The Silver Screen

The movies, perhaps even more than other entertainment, sustained people through the war. Cinemas were full from noon onwards, and audiences rarely left their seats for the shelters during air-raids. 'Cinemas now flash all clear! all clear! across the screen, regardless of the picture. It looked wonderful scrawled across Lillian Russell's 1880 bust,' reported *Vogue* in 1940. The war brought about significant improvements in the hitherto feeble state of British movies. While Hollywood continued in the main to cherish beliefs that good Box Office demanded love at first sight and a happy ending, lack of funds and an awakening sense of realities encouraged British film makers to produce entertainment that sustained and did not flagrantly rebut the experience of its war-stricken audience.

Noel Coward's first film epitomised the best of British war films. *In Which We Serve*, made in 1942 and co-directed by David Lean, told the story of a destroyer and her crew. It was inspired by the experience of Coward's friend Lord Louis Mountbatten, who was torpedoed off Crete. Mountbatten came with the King and Queen and the Princesses to visit the studios during filming. 'Coward has gauged the changing tempo with barometric accuracy and been successfully eloquent of the Twenties, Thirties, and now the early Forties,' wrote *Vogue*. 'His film is a wonderful and moving conception, or rather a reflection, of all that is greatest in the British spirit at war.' There were no big stars: Coward himself, John Mills, Celia Johnson, and Kay Walsh (David Lean's wife) acted with understatement and dignity, with the young Richard Attenborough giving a moving study of a wretched sailor who lost his nerve. Coward's long-standing art director, Gladys Calthrop, now a Commandant in the MTC, was released from her duties to work on the picture. *Vogue's* Lesley Blanch praised Coward's superb sense of restraint, of emphasis upon the British lack of emphasis, and expressed her 'profound relief to know that never, never would Veronica Lake pop up out of the conning tower, no matter how tough things became'.

There were countless other war films, all more or less tasteful propaganda: *Desert Victory*; *Western Approaches*; Carol Reed's *The Way Ahead* with David Niven; *Millions Like Us*, about women of all classes rubbing along together in the war effort. Leslie Howard directed *Pimpernel Smith*, in which he played an unassuming English traveller saving people from the Germans. He was also seen in *Forty-Ninth Parallel*, which *Vogue* called 'as eloquent of our creed as *Baptism of Fire* is of the Nazi ideology'. Eric Portman and John Mills starred in *They Dive at Dawn*, a submarine story, and Ralph Richardson was superb in *The Silver Fleet* as a Dutchman who sabotages his own shipyard when the Nazis take over. At the end of the war Sir Alexander Korda's comedy *Perfect Strangers* told with rueful realism the story of two young service people, now demobilised and grown apart by years of severed interests and separation.

Hollywood's eye-view of war was that of the English village in *Mrs Miniver,* with Greer Garson, and the nursing epic of Bataan, *So Proudly We Hail*, starring Veronica Lake, her much-copied peek-a-boo bob sheared to an ascetic crop. Tearjerkers like *The White Cliffs of Dover* made the English mad, and David Selznick's picture of the home front, *Since You Went Away*, was, wrote *Vogue*, 'stencilled emotions in a bag of banalities, a movie that collects details

Noel Coward and seven scenes
from "In Which We Serve"

1, Irish-born Greer Garson, 1948. PENN. *2,* Ann Todd and James Mason, stars of *The Seventh Veil,* 1945. *3,* Margaret Rutherford in *Passport to Pimlico,* 1949. *4,* Alec Guinness, 1947. LEE MILLER. *5,* Dirk Bogarde in *Esther Waters,* 1948. *6,* Richard Attenborough, promising young actor in *Brighton Rock,* 1947. COFFIN. *7,* Deborah Kerr, 1943. CECIL BEATON. *8,* Kay Hammond in the film version of Noel Coward's *Blithe Spirit,* 1944. *9,* the ghost of Hamlet's father, muffled in fog, and Sir Laurence Olivier as Hamlet, in his own film of the play, 1948

but understands nothing'. There was one film with a peripheral wartime theme that did capture people's hearts. It was *Casablanca* – 'built on the Grade B formula, carried to perfection' – with Humphrey Bogart, Ingrid Bergman as his old flame, and the toad-like Peter Lorre.

The US government recognised the importance of movies for propaganda purposes. Walt Disney, maker of *Fantasia, Bambi,* and *Pinocchio,* also brought out a couple of government shorts, *The New Spirit* and Major Alexander de Seversky's *Victory through Air Power,* in which cartoon characters slashed merrily at the Führer's face. Captain Clark Gable of the US Air Force, who saw active service on Antwerp bombing raids, made a training film entitled *Wings Up,* his voice good, raspy, and sexy.

With not much romance and glamour in everyday life, people wanted more than ever to see it on the screen. There were idols for every taste, sirens like Marlene Dietrich, the heavy-lidded enchantress (with insured legs) exuding slow-moving fascination in *The Spoiler* and *City of Sin.* Joan Crawford, 'the sort of Woman every Man Wants and Shouldn't Have', battled her way through the tense domestic drama *Mildred Pierce.* And Mae West: 'My undulations may be unorthodox, but the audience knows what I mean,' she told the press.

Newcomers included Bette Davis, Dorothy Lamour, and Betty Grable. Lauren Bacall, a wide-mouthed beauty with intelligent eyes, was discovered by Howard Hawks, who for weeks had her screaming lines from a hilltop into a headwind, until her voice dropped four tones into a sulky growl, sexy and curiously inviting. In 1945, 'too young and too old and entirely provocative', she began her lifelong partnership with the 44-year-old Humphrey Bogart in *To Have and To Hold.* Soon afterwards he was slapping her around in Raymond Chandler's *The Big Sleep.*

There were demure goddesses too, like the seraphic Deborah Kerr in *Major Barbara* and *Love on the Dole,* Ann Todd with her wide-spaced eyes in *Ships With Wings,* and Jennifer Jones, who played *The Song of Bernadette* with a sweet and dedicated gravity. Irish-born Greer Garson, who landed the coveted part of Mme Curie, retained her viola-voice and invincible ladylikeness even on the trapeze on which she had to swing in *Julia Misbehaves.* The Swedish beauty Ingrid Bergman had frightening stamina: her press agent reported that she neither smoked nor drank, and got staggering amounts of exercise and sleep. She was chosen by Hemingway to play the crop-haired Spanish country girl in his story of the Spanish Civil War, *For Whom the Bell Tolls,* with Gary Cooper. *Vogue* called it 'a technicolor war in a vacuum, almost without excitement, neither military nor amorous, even in its sleeping bag scene, of which someone said, too little and too late.'

Among the youngest screen goddesses were Elizabeth Taylor, the child star of *National Velvet,* later Amy in *Little Women;* the French teenager Anouk Aimée, playing in a modern-day version of the Romeo and Juliet story; and the snub-nosed, kittenish Jean Simmons. At eighteen she played Ophelia in Laurence Olivier's film version of *Hamlet.*

There were also men idols, and sometimes partnerships, like that of Spencer Tracy and Katharine Hepburn, who made nine films together. Gregory Peck made *The Keys of the Kingdom* (with Ingrid Bergman) and *Spellbound* and became the hottest acting property in Hollywood. New discovery Trevor Howard was seen in *The Way to the Stars* and with Celia Johnson in *Brief Encounter,* Noel Coward's tender love story set mainly in the buffet of a railway station. Henry Fonda, Burt Lancaster, James Stewart, Clark

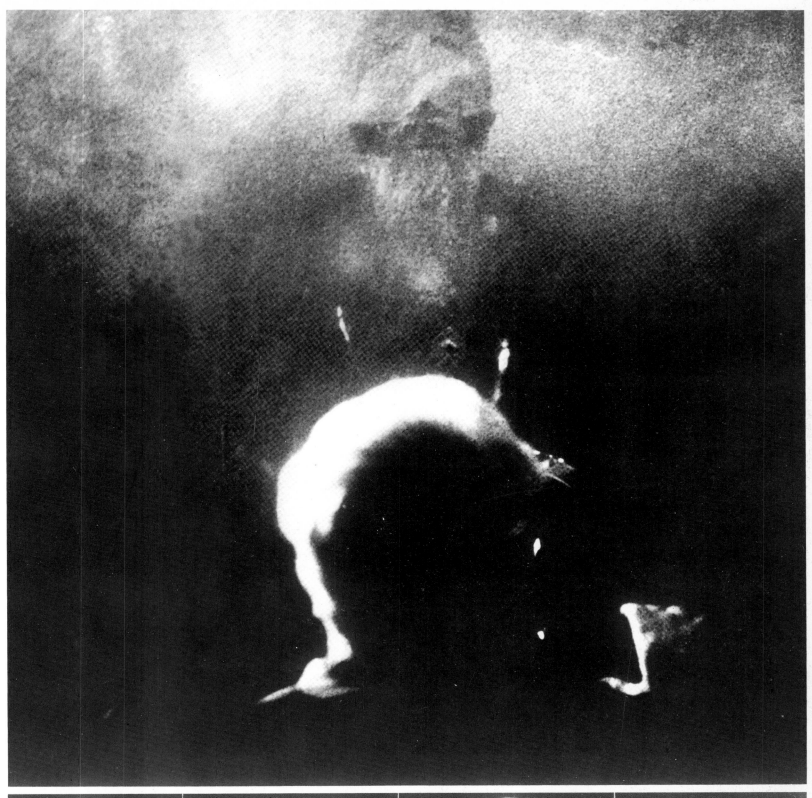

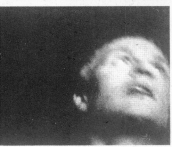

Gable, and David Niven joined up and missed a few years of movie-making, as did Laurence Olivier, who trained for the Fleet Air Arm. *Rebecca*, made in 1940, in which he played Max de Winter, with Joan Fontaine as his mousy wife, inspired a vogue for 'Rebecca mauve' and period clothes. The following year he acted Lord Nelson in *Lady Hamilton*, with his new wife Vivien Leigh in the title role. Winston Churchill saw the film four times, and cried each time at the Battle of Trafalgar.

For his debut as film producer, Olivier made *Henry V* in Technicolor – a milestone in Shakespearean cinema. 'Olivier is now the first man in English films,' declared *Vogue*. The action shifted effectively between a reconstructed Globe Theatre and re-enactments of the Battle of Agincourt, with Olivier, complete with medieval haircut, playing Henry. Two years later, in 1948, he produced, directed, and starred in his black and white film of *Hamlet*, for which William Walton provided a brassy score.

Vivien Leigh had shot to stardom in 1939 as the tough Scarlett in *Gone With The Wind*, which played exclusively at the Ritz, Leicester Square, for three years. She soon found herself playing a variety of different roles: a vulnerable ballerina in *Waterloo Bridge*, Anna in Korda's *Anna Karenina* (Anouilh wrote the scenario, and Cecil Beaton designed the costumes), and the vixenish Cleopatra in Bernard Shaw's much-publicised *Caesar and Cleopatra*. In the latter she worked alongside Claude Rains as Caesar and Flora Robson as the bossy Ftatateeta, dressed in costumes by Oliver Messel. Shaw had finally consented to allow the filming of his plays by the Hungarian director Gabriel Pascal. In 1941 another of these, *Major Barbara*, with its ironically apposite theme, god or armaments, was completed at Denham, despite the chaos wreaked by the blitz. Some of the stars, including Wendy Hiller and Penelope Dudley-Ward, holed up in their dressing rooms for the duration.

Another controversial, all-round man of the cinema was Orson Welles. 'Welles is legendary: an outsize *enfant terrible*: a titanesque tycoon. Everything about him is outrageous, splendid, remarkable . . . Welles is sloppy, greedy, brilliant, six foot three, and married to Rita Hayworth . . . He is said to be the genius of the age, or a fraud.' *Citizen Kane*, which he wrote and directed, as well as playing its title role, was based on a brilliant bitter biography of William Randolph Hearst. Its self-conscious artistry, with all sorts of tricks – tipped cameras, crazy distortions, furious montages, big foregrounds, and distant horizons – served to make audiences more aware of cinematic technique. Welles also acted in Graham Greene's thriller *The Third Man*. Directed by Carol Reed with superb technique and control, the film counterpointed the closely observed characters and the character of the sad city of Vienna, to an accompaniment of haunting zither music.

Earlier, Reed's film of H.G. Wells's *Kipps*, with Michael Redgrave as the lovable hero, was widely acclaimed. Other British directors also made memorable films. David Lean, 'that prophet with such overwhelming honour in his own country, the cutting room,' made two enduring classics: *Great Expectations*, with Martita Hunt as Miss Haversham, and *Oliver Twist*, with Alec Guinness brilliant as Fagin (and exciting the disapproval of the American Board of Rabbis), the gamine Kay Walsh as Nancy, and the young Anthony Newley as the Artful Dodger.

Alfred Hitchcock, that master of suspense and apprehension, made his first Technicolor film, *The Rope*, in 1948. For it he used a camera specially built on an electric dolly, referred to by some of his crew as Hitch's Pony Express. Another name to watch was that of the extraordinary young Peter Ustinov, son of the painter

1, Ingrid Bergman and Gary Cooper in *For Whom the Bell Tolls,* 1943. BALKIN. *2,* Katharine Hepburn, 1943. VANDAMM. *3,* Spencer Tracy, 1948. PENN. *4,* Gregory Peck, 'the hottest acting property in Hollywood', 1945. *5,* Dorothy Lamour, 1942. *6,* Loretta Young and turban, 1940. RAWLINGS. *7,* Judy Garland, star of *Meet Me in St Louis,* 1945. *8,* Veronica Lake, star of *Star Spangled Rhythm,* 1942. *9,* Lauren Bacall, 1945. CRANE

Nadia Benois. He showed his satirical wit and perceptive eye in several films, including *School for Secrets*, about the discovery and development of radar, the comic fantasy *Vice Versa*, and *Private Angelo*. 'He has all of Coward's brilliant sleight of hand and an imagination that will carry him a good deal further,' wrote *Vogue*.

Important American directors included documentary-maker Robert Flaherty, who made the sensitive *Louisiana Story*, and John Huston, whose version of the Pardoner's Tale, *The Treasure of the Sierra Madre*, was sparely photographed, with nervous and cleverly sardonic dialogue. John Ford directed Henry Fonda as Tom in *The Grapes of Wrath*, Steinbeck's 'great, depressing saga of discomfort and despair'.

The French cinema, which had been pre-eminent in Europe before the war, inevitably suffered under the Occupation. The Nazis tried to force many French actors to make conciliatory films showing the Germans and French in happy union. A few collaborated, among them Arletty and Sacha Guitry, but many fled, including Jean Gabin, who escaped to America and the arms of Twentieth Century-Fox. Only after the war were films by the great French directors seen in Britain. Anna Magnani gave a virtuoso performance on screen in Jean Cocteau's *La Voix Humaine*, the monologue of an abandoned woman listening to her lover's voice on the phone. But Cocteau's macabre and magical *La Belle et la Bête* bored and depressed *Vogue*'s reviewer Siriol Hugh Jones by its 'hollow monotony'. *The Chips are Down*, a strange, harshly photographed film written by Jean-Paul Sartre, about a rich woman and a revolutionary workman who meet and fall in love after death, again showed Sartre's intense and pessimistic preoccupation with what happens after death.

The postwar Italian cinema flowered with the neo-realists Vittorio de Sica (*The Bicycle Thieves*), Roberto Rossellini (*Germany Year Zero*), and Alberto Lattuada (*Without Pity*). These directors preferred to improvise their scripts and to use non-professional actors, and made films showing the daily brutalities facing most Italians. Rossellini used the actress Ingrid Bergman for his film *Stromboli*, and their partnership flowered into a seven-year marriage.

But all was not unrelieved seriousness. The Marx Brothers gave us *A Night in Casablanca* and *Love Happy*. Chaplin made his satirical *The Great Dictator*, about a Jewish barber who resembled Hitler. Margaret Rutherford was very funny in *Passport to Pimlico*, about a London district that wanted to secede from Britain. Jacques Tati convulsed audiences in his movie debut *Jour de Fête*, and Rex Harrison was properly offhand about his rather difficult marital problems in *Blithe Spirit*.

In 1947, the Chancellor of the Exchequer, Dr Hugh Dalton, almost ruined the British film industry by slapping a 75 per cent tax on all imported films. Hollywood retaliated by suspending shipment of all films, and British companies started churning out hastily made films to fill the gap. A few months later, when the tax was lifted by the President of the Board of Trade, Harold Wilson, no-one wanted to see them, and companies like Rank lost millions.

1. Anna Magnani in the film of Cocteau's *La Voix Humaine*, 1947. *2.* Anouk Aimée, teenage star of a modern-day *Romeo and Juliet*, 1948. *3.* Jacques Tati as the postman in *Jour de Fête*, 1949. DOISNEAU. *4.* Gérard Philippe, already a name in France, 1948. *5.* Françoise Rosay, actress wife of director Jacques Feyder, 1943. CECIL BEATON. *6.* Danièle Delorme, 1949. *7.* Jean Gabin, famous star of *La Grande Illusion* and *Pépé Le Moko*, 1941. RAWLINGS

Clip from Vittorio de Sica's *The Bicycle Thieves*, 1949

1, Roberto Rossellini, Italian 'neo-realist' director, 1949. *2,* Alfred Hitchcock in 1948, when he was making his first Techni-color movie, *The Rope.* PENN. *3,* Vittorio de Sica, eminent Italian director, 1949. *4,* David Lean directing night shooting on *Oliver Twist,* 1948. *5,* the Boulting Brothers, sketched by Bouché, 1947. *6,* director Carol Reed studying the model of Folkestone pier built for trick shots for his film *Kipps,* 1941. CECIL BEATON. *7, Vogue's* 'symbolist' portrait of Orson Welles, 1946. 'The Doré *Inferno* engraving suggests his hell-fire intensity; the raven, his voice of doom. The French horn, plums, port wine – his fruitiness; the beer and the beach ball – his heavy bounce. The old camera, gramophone celluloid collar – his archaic tinge. The silk hat, his magical showmanship. The firecracker, hoop, electric train – his *enfant terrible* intelligence.' PENN

Opposite, Matisse working in bed on designs for the Vence chapel, and *above,* his charcoal sketches, 1949. COFFIN

Art and Artists

The artistic treasures of Britain and America were sent into hiding because of the war. The National Gallery's collection was shipped off to a temperature-controlled cave at Bodnant in Wales, while those of the Metropolitan Museum were stored outside Philadelphia in Whitemarch Hall, the mansion belonging to socialite Mrs Stotesbury. The magnificent Sutton Hoo Viking ship and its hoard of Byzantine silver and jewels, discovered in Suffolk just before war broke out, was hidden in Aldwych underground station and not seen by the public until 1946.

However, the National Gallery, under its director Sir Kenneth Clark, did not close: indeed it became the focal point of the nation's cultural life. It held War Artist shows and weekly lunchtime concerts, which were the brainchild of Myra Hess. If you didn't take sandwiches you could buy your lunch in the canteen. As the war progressed, the Gallery also dared to hang a single Picture of the Month, which always drew an appreciative crowd

– among these works were El Greco's *Christ and the Moneylenders* and the Rokeby *Venus.*

The indefatigable Sir Kenneth also organized the War Artists' Scheme, setting artists to record the war. This was a task that took them completely outside their usual environment and scope. Stanley Spencer was sent to record shipbuilding on the Clyde. Illustrator Feliks Topolski, who worked regularly for *Vogue,* toured the battle fronts and brought home pictures of destruction and homelessness. Paul Nash, who had also recorded the First World War, painted the Battle of Britain. Stage designer Oliver Messel and architect Basil Spence designed camouflage for the army. In an imaginative film entitled *Out of Chaos,* film-maker Jill Craigie recorded the work and thoughts of many war painters. Most agreed that the impact of war was to lead them away from abstract and surrealist tendencies towards a more personal expression of their mind's eye – seen imaginatively, in the works of Paul Nash.

The sculptor Henry Moore, who was already considered England's greatest artist, produced a moving record of life in air-raid shelters and coalmines. 'The first emotion excited by a Moore carving is likely to be disquietude, even alarm,' Raymond Mortimer told *Vogue* readers. He went on to praise Moore's war work. 'Some of these coloured drawings – he has a very personal sense of colour – might be illustrations for Dante's *Inferno*: long perspectives of recumbent figures pressed shoulder to shoulder and thigh to thigh, cruelly without privacy in a claustrophobic underworld; men and women asleep beside their children, reminding us of Mantegna by their anguished and foreshortened heads and the folds that mould their uneasy frames. No realism here; yet no other artist in any country has, so far as I know, come near to expressing so fully the pity inspired by the victims of scientific war.'

Vogue also featured articles championing the work of other British artists, including Graham Sutherland, John Piper, Matthew Smith, and Frances Hodgkins.

'That sombrero'd scallywag, that flamboyant Welsh gypsy genius' Augustus John – or 'Disgustus John', as George V had called him – was commissioned to paint a portrait of the Queen. *Vogue* published an early sketch, describing it as 'a violent break with the rather sycophantic tradition of Court portraiture'.

Many European artists escaped to America, including Chagall, Amédée Ozenfant, Max Ernst, and Fernand Léger, who painted the confused bodies he saw while waiting on the Marseilles beaches in 1940 in a series of works called *Man and Space*. Max Jacob died in a concentration camp; *Vogue* published a memorial tribute to him. Other artists stoically stayed put: Picasso refused to leave Paris and was discovered in his studio by Lee Miller when she entered the liberated city with the American army. Matisse remained at Vence, bedridden after an operation in 1941, looking after his collection of caged birds (depleted by the war from 300 to seventy) and illustrating surrealist poems by the Maquis leader René Char. Later in the decade he devoted himself to designing the chapel Sainte Marie du Rosaire. He not only worked on the windows and murals, but conceived the whole structure – the first of his generation of painters to venture into architecture.

America was growing ever more receptive to 'modern art'. The Museum of Modern Art held a successful exhibition of mobile sculpture by Alexander Calder, and in 1944, fifteen years after its opening, it mounted a huge retrospective of modern painting, which was described as a complete education in modern art. Peggy Guggenheim, who was married to Max Ernst and once said, 'This is the age of collection, not of creation,' showed the work of many up-and-coming artists, including 'abstract expressionists' like 'Jack the Dripper' Jackson Pollock.

Meanwhile the Museum of Non-Objective Art, founded in 1939, also drew its share of cynical quips. 'Only those in front of the publicised international *avant-garde* go to its galleries on Fifth Avenue,' wrote *Vogue*. 'Although some of the paintings are incomprehensible even to the initiates, the scoffers are often charmed by the colours and shapes. Psychiatry majors often go to this haven for dreamers of extremely modern dreams.' Frank Lloyd Wright was commissioned to design a building to house the Museum, and his plans for a circular, fantastic 'Assyrian ziggurat' with a ten-storey ramp caused much excitement.

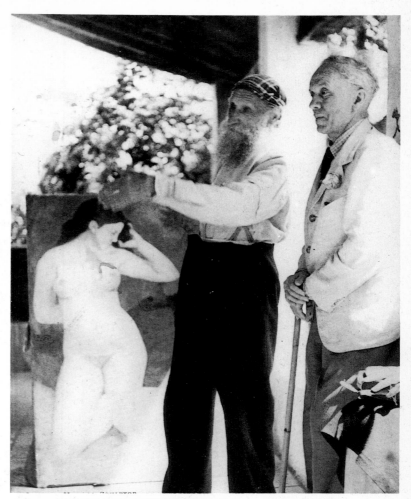

Opposite, the painter Richard Sickert and his wife, 1941. CECIL BEATON. *Above right,* the sculptor Aristide Maillol with painter Raoul Dufy, 1942. *Right,* Marc Chagall, having left Paris for New York, 1942. HERMANN

1

1, Henry Moore with Three Standing Figures in Battersea Park, 1948. PARKINSON. *2,* the painter Balthus, 1949. *3,* the New Zealand artist Frances Hodgkins, 1947. *4,* Scottish painter Robert Colquhoun, 1946. *5,* Graham Sutherland with his model Somerset Maugham, 1949. CECIL BEATON. *6,* Paul Nash, official war artist, at a salvage dump, 1944. *7,* Fernand Léger, 1949. DOISNEAU. *8,* Giorgio de Chirico, 1946. *9,* André Dérain, 1949. PENN. *10,* Stanley Spencer, war artist, sketching in a shipyard, 1944

131

Books and Book Reviews

'Bookshops are so crammed, jammed, full that you can rarely get near the shelves,' wrote *Vogue* in 1943. 'And if you do, it is difficult to find the book you want. Editions of the latest novels and biographies are limited and sell out fast. The classics are in great demand and even harder to get, for soldiers going overseas take them as an essential part of their embarkation kit; and civilians buy them as an investment. Their scarcity value rises daily, and classics are really worth their weight in money.' No-one wanted to read about war or politics, and even thrillers paled before contemporary events. Cecil Beaton wrote: 'Rather than "go out" with "anyone", people are content to spend evenings alone with the masters of great literature. Tolstoy's *War and Peace* is sold out all over England.' Delighted publishers could have sold their stocks many times over, but were unable to capitalise on their good fortune because of paper shortages.

Vogue nourished this need for books with news and reviews of the latest and greatest in literature. It ran profiles of writers, including Isherwood and Huxley in California, and Evelyn Waugh ('Tory with Laughs'), who had just published *The Loved One*. Peter Quennell described the work of Ivy Compton-Burnett, V.S. Pritchett, and Henry Green. Alan Paton wrote of South Africa, the setting for his novel *Cry, the Beloved Country*. French *Vogue* published an excerpt of *Other Voices, Other Rooms*, by the exciting newcomer Truman Capote. Lee Miller described how on entering Paris with the liberating army she went to visit Colette and found her writing in bed, as usual. Cecil Beaton also visited Paris and photographed Parisian literary lights. Jean-Paul Sartre gave his views on 'New Writing in France', and Diana Trilling contributed a piece entitled 'Ideas to Watch in Books'. *Vogue* also brought the work of the Italians Moravia, Levi, and Silone to readers' attention.

In 1948 T.S. Eliot, 'the literary conscience of an era', was awarded the Nobel Prize. The previous year saw the publication of W.H. Auden's *The Age of Anxiety*, a poem which took place mostly in a Manhattan bar and told incisively about:

> *a land of glass*
> *Where song is grimace, sound logic*
> *A suite of gestures*

But the most important literary movement to come out of the experience of war was that of existentialism. Its chief exponent was the young Albert Camus, author of *L'Etranger* and the play *Caligula*. Like many young French writers, he had worked in the Resistance, where the constant presence of death and the perpetual threat of torture had forced his awareness of the powers and limits of man. Camus himself explained his philosophy in *Vogue* in an article entitled 'The Crisis of Man'. Although life is absurd, he argued, fear is the great enemy: 'The strongest temptation of man is the temptation of inertia . . . But the truth remains that no man can die in peace if he has not at least once questioned his life and the lives of others – if he has not done what he can for the possible peace of mankind . . . Today what we need is a folly of man. A great, far-thinking, sound folly built on the immense hope, the silent determination which has sustained in the past and will continue to sustain some European minds in a world they have faced without benefit of illusion. When one knows this, perhaps it is easier to answer the question, are we pessimists?'

1. T.S. Eliot, 'the literary conscience of an era', 1947. LEE MILLER. **2.** novelist Ivy Compton-Burnett, 1949. CECIL BEATON. **3.** poet Stephen Spender, 1947. LEE MILLER. **4.** Ignazio Silone, Italian anti-Fascist writer, 1946. COFFIN. **5.** Welsh poet Dylan Thomas, author of *Death and Entrances*, 1947. LEE MILLER. **6.** André Gide, 1945. CECIL BEATON. **7.** poet Cecil Day Lewis, 1942. CECIL BEATON. **8.** Arthur Koestler, author of *Darkness at Noon*, 1946

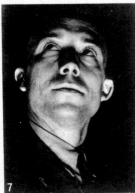

TITUS GROAN by Mervyn Peake, 1946

The most remarkable, exciting and individual novel published for some years is *Titus Groan*, written by the artist Mervyn Peake and published by Eyre and Spottiswoode – oddly enough, without the obvious illustrations. It is a piece of highly coloured imaginative writing which took the author seven years to complete – and the extravagant happenings that take place in the fantastic yet very real stronghold of Gormenghast bear some relation to the writing of Peacock, with none of Peacock's light-hearted satirical purpose. Mr Peake's prose has the alarming vividness and individuality of his drawing, and I have not met anything quite like Dr Prunesquallor and Lady Fuchsia Groan this side of nightmare for unavoidable memorability.

THIEVES IN THE NIGHT by Arthur Koestler, 1946

Arthur Koestler possesses the kind of penetrating international mind that pokes around in the problems of the times he is living in. With a news sense that many a journalist would prize, Koestler has managed in the last few years to hit the book stores with a novel analysing in terms of characters the very events that the newspapers are headlining. Just as Palestine is staying on the front pages, Koestler's newest book is a novel of Jews, Arabs, and British officials. By far the best of Koestler lies in his historical sense, definitely not in his characterisations. Once a Communist living in Russia, Koestler has never recovered from his own disillusionment, and gnaws away at Communism in practically everything he writes.

THE DEMON LOVER by Elizabeth Bowen, 1946

A volume of short stories by Elizabeth Bowen, *The Demon Lover* overwhelms detachment, so that, instead of observing from the outside what she is describing, we find that we are going up the stairs with her character in the half-blitzed house and following her again out into the street. Though sometimes a full view of her human beings is neglected, nevertheless she is one of our most gifted writers, and in these new stories, where the subconscious materialises its own ghosts, she is at her best.

NINETEEN EIGHTY FOUR by George Orwell, 1949

The theme of Mr George Orwell's book is the defeat of the spirit of man. 'Stamping for ever on the human face' is the idea with which he regales himself and dire indeed is the picture he gives of the life we shall shortly be living – if we do not mend our ways. And what hope has Mr Orwell ever given us that man will mend his ways? Is not his whole philosophy based on the belief that Good is weak and Evil all-powerful, and is he not now, in the exercise of his sombre talent, horrifying himself in a delicious way with the fruits of that glum faith? In this book the little virtue that is left to man is ill-vested in Winston Smith, a poor weak creature who is a good deal weaker when the secret Police have finished torturing him in their Ministry of Love. It is perhaps a pity that Mr Orwell writes about people at all. He is a pure intellectual and should write about ideas. *Stevie Smith*

1, novelist Elizabeth Bowen, 1945. *2,* Evelyn Waugh, author of *Brideshead Revisited*, 1945. *3,* playwright Tennessee Williams, 1945. *4,* Cyril Connolly, fastidious writer, critic, and editor of *Horizon*, 1945. CECIL BEATON. *5,* Carson McCullers, *enfant terrible* of American letters, 1943. *6,* Truman Capote, author of *Other Voices, Other Rooms*, 1949. COFFIN. *7,* Albert Camus, existentialist philosopher, lecturer, playwright, and novelist, 1946. CECIL BEATON. *8,* Jean-Paul Sartre, exponent of existentialism, 1946

_1._ Aldous Huxley at the window of his Californian desert home, 1947. He left England to live in America before the outbreak of war. _2._ Christopher Isherwood, also in self-imposed exile in California, 1947. _3._ George Orwell, author of _1984_ and _Animal Farm_, 1946. _4._ Vladimir Nabokov, Russian emigré author, 1947

The Kitchen Front

'Throughout England, cooking is topic A in conversation,' wrote *Vogue* in 1942. 'Having learnt to cook lately is not a handicap – you don't miss the dollop of butter, pint of cream and half dozen eggs that pre-war cooks flung in haphazardly. Harrods' grocery department holds a cooking demonstration every afternoon from 3 to 4, where you can pick up hundreds of hints on making the most of your food.'

Rationing meant, throughout the decade, 2–3 oz tea a week, 8–16 oz sugar, 1–8 oz cheese, 2–8 oz bacon, 4–8 oz butter and margarine. There was a national loaf, and, if you were lucky, one egg a fortnight. There were no onions or bananas, but the British were introduced to spam (spiced ham) and dried eggs. Meat was the most problematic: you were allowed at the worst stage, in 1949 and 1951, 10d worth – 8d worth of 'carcass meat' and 2d worth of corned beef. Whale meat proved fairly acceptable; not so a fish called snoek from South Africa. The name itself was a comedian's delight, and the public eschewed it in any form. It was eventually sold off as catfood.

Rationing got worse, not better, when the war ended. Nevertheless, many people actually ate better during the war than before because of the strict control of food. With restaurant prices pegged at five shillings a meal, many people who had never been inside a restaurant before started to eat out. The problem was making interesting meals out of the endless plentiful starch. 'Potato dishes have burst into favour with the war,' *Vogue* wrote in 1940: needs must. The government took space in magazines to show people how to make omelettes out of dried egg and to use familiar things in novel ways: 'Shredded cabbage in salads – a new taste thrill.' It also suggested having one or more meatless days a week.

Hoarding and misusing rations and blackmarketing were severely frowned on as treacherous, although everyone was supposed to store one week's food supply and become 'a small self-reliant fortress within the great fortress that is Britain'. 'A loaded board of rich foods, if they could be obtained "somehow", would be as vulgar as the three beds in the vulgar story of the parvenu couple,' wrote Cecil Beaton in 1942. 'Austerity meals make everyone laugh,' echoed *Vogue* on another occasion. 'Lord Woolton [the Minister of Food] urges us to lick out the jamjar, to scrape the plate. We do so with gusto, and table-manners begin to change accordingly.' People talk longingly of oranges and lemons, which were not seen for the duration, and dreamt about meals they would order after the war.

Vogue was full of its own hints for cooks, as well as suggesting cookery books such as Ambrose Heath's *Kitchen Front Recipes* and *Eating Well in Wartime* by Leonora Eyles. Constance Spry told *Vogue* readers how to grow vegetables in flower borders and herbs and tomatoes in window boxes. The magazine was full of recipes to help with the problems of rationing: minimum meat recipes, no-meat recipes of pasta, soufflés, and pancakes, desserts without sugar, and salad dressings without oil or eggs (one dressing used reconstituted custard powder). 'Put banal meat-followed-by-sweet ideas right out of your head,' *Vogue* suggested. 'So long as your main dish is substantial, your secondary course, whether served before or after, can be as unconventional as you please.'

To cheer people up, *Vogue* encouraged a revival of teatime. It showed ladies such as Mrs Winston Churchill, Lady Maureen

1, life must go on: Mrs Winston Churchill taking tea in her private sitting room at No. 10, 1940. *2,* international hostess the Duchess of Windsor in consultation with her chef in her Paris house, 1949. The photograph accompanied an article she wrote for *Vogue* entitled 'When I Entertain'. CECIL BEATON. *3,* and *4,* more tea-drinkers: the Hon Mrs Peter Rodd, otherwise Nancy Mitford, presiding over her Mappin and Webb silver service, and Lady Maureen Stanley, wife of the War Minister, 1940

Precious CRUSTS

No scrap of bread is too small to save — it means saving valuable shipping space. Of course your best and most direct way of helping, is to take less bread into the house. Most households find they can do nicely with three-quarters of the bread they used to buy and yet can give every member of the family all the bread he or she individually needs.

The secret is in eating up every scrap of bread that comes in. Don't forget the end of the loaf. It's the bit that's apt to get left over. You always intended to do something with it. But how often was it thrown out, after all!

Half a slice of stale bread saved by everyone in this country every day, means a convoy of 30 ships a year freed to take munitions or men to our fighting fronts. If you explain this to your family you'll find them eager enough to help you save on bread!

> ### Save Bread: Save Ships
> #### 4 things you can do
> 1 Cut down your purchase (or making) of bread. Most households find they can do nicely with three-quarters of the bread they used to buy.
>
> 2 Put the loaf on the dresser or side table. Cut only as required.
>
> 3 Use every crumb.
>
> 4 Don't eat bread whilst potatoes are on the table.

Some ways of using up STALE BREAD

CRISPY PIE-CRUST. Cut bread into dice ¼ in. thick. Cover a savoury pie with them, setting the dice closely together. Pour over them a little thin custard (salted) taking care that every piece of bread is moistened. Bake in a brisk oven.

SOAKED BREAD. This is the foundation of a countless number of puddings and cakes. No bread is too stale for it, and there is no need to remove any crust. Break into small pieces, put into bowl, cover completely with cold water and soak thoroughly. If the bread is to be used for a savoury, use vegetable boilings instead of water. Then squeeze the bread *hard*, put back in the bowl and beat with a fork until quite free from lumps and pieces of crust. The beating is most important and makes all the difference between a dull heavy pudding and a smooth, spongy texture.

MINCE SLICES. Mix 8 ozs. mince with 4 ozs. cooked mashed potatoes and 4 ozs. fine crumbs. Season to taste. Roll out on a floured board into an oblong ¼ in. thick. Cut into slices and fry in a very little hot fat or grill for 5 to 7 minutes. Serve with leek sauce.

MAKING RUSKS. Cut bread into neat figures, or fancy shapes, about ¼ in. thick. Bake in a warm oven until crisp and golden brown. Pack in an air-tight tin. This is a valuable emergency store which will keep good for months.

TURN WASTE INTO DELICACIES!

ISSUED BY THE MINISTRY OF FOOD (S61)

Stanley (wife of the Minister for War) and Mrs Peter Rodd (otherwise Nancy Mitford) wielding comforting silver services from Mappin and Webb in their safely blacked-out chintz drawing rooms, and published their recipes for brioches and cakes. However, 'for the benefit of those who have been struggling with wartime worries in the form of red tape or red tabs, there will lurk an adjacent table, loaded with decanters'.

Many ladies, losing their servants to the factories, took cookery lessons. (Diane Lucas, cookery correspondent of American *Vogue*, ran her own cooking school.) After the war, even had it been possible to return to the old ways, these ladies were often content to keep control of the kitchen. There were significant labour-saving developments to help them. Doris Lytton Toye, British *Vogue*'s cookery reporter, wrote in 1948: 'Quick freeze methods have come to stay, turning our bill of winter fare topsy-turvy... Having just visited a bewildering display of frozen food in a glass case somehow reminiscent of an aquarium, I know how many varieties of fruit and vegetables can be frozen.' Another new invention was the pressure cooker. 'You couldn't blow yourself up with it if you tried,' Mrs Toye reassured more timorous readers. Here are some of *Vogue's* suggestions for economical and minimum-meat dishes:

STUFFED CABBAGE. 1 lb minced beef, 4 thick slices of bread, 1 egg, 2 lb cabbage, ½ pint milk, a little finely minced onion or leek, salt and pepper. Cut the crusts from the bread and soak it in the milk, add the meat, salt, pepper (or teaspoon of paprika), onion and the beaten egg. Mix well. Separate the leaves of the cabbage. Cook for five minutes in boiling salted water and drain. Fill each leaf with a tablespoon of the mixture, roll over and fill a fireproof dish, so that the rolls are tightly pressed together. Add a little water and 2 oz fat. Bake in a hot oven for half an hour. Make a sauce by thickening the liquid in the pan — add more water if it has lessened in cooking — and flavour with tomato sauce. Pour this over the rolls and bake for another ten minutes. Serve with boiled potatoes. If using left-over meat, cooked rice is better than the soaked bread. Regulo Mark 6.

POLENTA WITH SAUSAGE. Stir a pound of cornflour, a little at a time, into a pint of boiling salted water until smooth. Put a layer half an inch thick on a board to cool. When quite cold cut it into pieces an inch long. Place a layer of these in a fireproof dish, sprinkle with cheese (parmesan if you have it) and cover with small pieces of skinned and boiled sausage, moistened with tomato purée or sauce. Repeat the layers until the dish is full, dotting each layer with small bits of margarine. Cook in the oven and serve very hot. Regulo Mark 5.

MUTTON PIES. 1 lb lean mutton, ¼ lb mushrooms, 3 shallots, parsley, puff pastry, flour for thickening. Dice the mutton, mix with the chopped mushrooms, parsley and shallots and season with pepper and salt. Put in a saucepan, barely cover with water or stock, and cook for about an hour, then thicken with a little flour and let get cold. Take some patty pans the size of a small saucer and line with puff pastry. Fill with the meat mixture, place a cover of the pastry on each, make a hole in the centre with a skewer, brush the top with beaten egg or milk, and bake till brown. Serve with stewed watercress to which a little vinegar has been added. Regulo Mark 8.

Opposite, actor Alfred Lunt teaching his cooking class at the Algonquin Hotel in New York, in aid of the American Theatre Wing War Service, 1942. Drawing by Eric

Music Notes

'Throughout the last six years in France, there has been new music – and a new audience for it,' wrote Nadia Boulanger in *Vogue* in 1946. 'It is an enthusiastic audience, attentive and full of curiosity. It has packed the many concerts – for the comfort of music, the comfort of being together.' The Paris Conservatory never closed its doors under the Occupation: its Director made false identification papers for his students and managed to keep them from being deported to Germany. The composer Georges Auric refused to present any of his music in France, although his enchanting film scores for *Caesar and Cleopatra* and René Clair's *A Nous La Liberté* were enjoyed in England and America.

In England a bomb wiped out the Queen's Hall, and Sir Henry Wood's Promenade concerts eventually found a new home at the Albert Hall. Covent Garden did its bit for the war by becoming a dance hall. Dame Myra Hess's bob-a-lunchtime concerts at the National Gallery were enormously popular: 'A real cross-section of Britain – from the Queen to the typist at the Ministry of Information – can be seen, munching their sandwich lunch, and listening to Bach, Mozart, and Brahms.' Famous musicians were given short leave from their military duties to play.

Vogue displayed a wide musical interest. One frequent contributor was Virgil Thomson, who, in an article entitled 'Ideas to Watch in Music' in 1949, told readers that the modernist war was drawing to a close and 'even tonality now enjoys some tolerance'. Audiences were judging works by their content and not their syntax. (This in contrast to the advice of Gerald F. Warburg in another article: 'Don't say you like modern music – nobody does.') Thomson predicted that television would have a major effect on music. Toscanini was among the first to adopt the new medium, when he conducted *Aïda* on television in 1949.

Vogue also ran articles on many world-renowned musicians, including the Finnish composer Jean Sibelius, and the fiery Toscanini at rehearsal. The Maestro, who conducted two hundred musicians in an enormous concert of Wagner and Verdi at Madison Square Gardens, was invited back to the Italy he had renounced in the early Thirties to give a series of concerts in aid of rebuilding La Scala. In 1943, the magazine published an interview with Rachmaninov – just before his death – to celebrate fifty years of performing. 'The seed of the future music of America lies in Negro music,' said the composer. 'What character there is in it to work with!'

Shostakovitch wrote the first important piece of music inspired by the war: his Seventh Symphony was composed in 1941 during the siege of Leningrad and smuggled to America on microfilm. Arthur Rubinstein, known offstage as Ruby, toured America in 1943 and was pronounced 'the most entertaining man in town'; his wife was labelled the best cook in Hollywood.

W.H. Auden, self-confessed opera addict, explained the delights of the genre to *Vogue* readers. Auden was working with Stravinsky on an opera entitled *The Rake's Progress*, based on the Hogarth drawings of a London rake.

One of the most noted names in America was that of Aaron Copland, composer of *Appalachian Spring*. *Vogue* reported that in 1945 six of the big symphony orchestras started their seasons with Copland compositions. Another name was that of conductor Leonard Bernstein. A former pupil of Koussevitsky, he was inter-

Opposite, Arthur Rubinstein playing Manuel de Falla's *The Fire Dance,* 'the music for which he is most famous', 1944. GJON MILI. *Above,* influential composer Igor Stravinsky, collaborator with W.H. Auden on the opera *The Rake's Progress,* 1948. PENN

ested in all sorts of music, even jazz, and composed scores for the musical *On The Town* and the ballet *Fancy Free*. In 1943, when he was 25 years old, he substituted at a few hours' notice for Bruno Walter on the podium of the New York Philharmonic, and took the critics by storm. Two years later he was invited to be conductor of the New York City Symphony Orchestra. 'The New York City Orchestra under Leonard Bernstein has turned Monday evening and Tuesday afternoon performances into both social success and musical excitement with his young instrumentalists, some still in uniform,' *Vogue* reported in 1945.

Harmonica player Larry Adler also gained tremendous acclaim: Darius Milhaud wrote a harmonica solo especially for him, which he performed with the French National Orchestra.

In England, *Peter Grimes* (1945), an opera about a psychologically disturbed Suffolk fisherman, was hailed as 'the most significant fact in the history of English music'. It was written by the 32-year-old Suffolk-born Benjamin Britten, who had been composing since the age of eight. Britten, wrote *Vogue*, 'is a shy, agreeable, thin young man with a certain young rabbity timidity at first appearance, but with the ferocity of a starved cannibal about his convictions'. Peter Grimes was sung by the tenor Peter Pears.

Sir Arthur Bliss and the self-taught Michael Tippett were also working on new operas. Elisabeth Lutyens, daughter of Sir Edwin Lutyens, was known for her atonal music, including a 'dramatic scene' in praise of the British miner, called *The Pit*. Lutyens was chosen to represent Britain at the Festival of Contemporary Music, and also composed the music for the 2000th anniversary of Julius Caesar's conquest of Britain, dramatised by Louis MacNiece.

The Royal Philharmonic Society now had an orchestra of its own, founded by Sir Thomas Beecham – the eighth orchestra he had founded. It rather defiantly opened its career with a series of concerts in Croydon. 'I am told they are a very good audience in Croydon,' said Sir Thomas. The irascible old conductor wrote an article for *Vogue* entitled 'Women *Ruin* Music', which ended: 'I do not like, and never will, the association of men and women in orchestras and other instrumental combinations. My spirit is torn all the time between a natural inclination to let myself go and the depressing thought that I must behave like a little gentleman. I have been unable to avoid noticing that the presence of half a dozen good-looking women in the orchestra is a distinctly distracting factor. As a member of the orchestra once said to me, "If she is attractive I can't play with her, and if she is not then I won't."'

Newcomers included Kathleen Ferrier, the young Lancashire contralto who had worked as a telephone operator and never had a singing lesson till she was 25, and Geraint Evans, who was first heard at Covent Garden in *Die Meistersinger* in 1948.

The most exciting happening on the British musical scene was the Edinburgh Festival of Music and Drama. Inspired by the Salzburg Festival, it was founded in 1947 by the Glyndebourne Opera Company's Rudolph Bing. Kathleen Ferrier, Bruno Walter, Lotte Lehmann, Todd Duncan, William Primrose, and Carl Ebert were among those who appeared in its inaugural year. By 1949 it was attracting 300,000 people and had become Britain's leading cultural event. *Vogue* wrote in 1948 of 'hordes of mid-European music lovers consuming all the fish teas . . . The Minister of Fuel and Power reconsidered a rude refusal to grant a permit for the castle to be illuminated, and vast numbers of locals and Sassenachs regaled themselves with such diversions as Jouvet in Giraudoux, Walter conducting Mahler, ballroom dancing beneath the Scott memorial, floodlit pipers and a "floral clock".'

Top, Finnish composer Jean Sibelius, characteristically dressed in a white suit with inevitable cigar, 1940. *Above,* composer Darius Milhaud, one of the members of the group Les Six, in 1949, when he returned to France after having spent seven years in America. PENN

Above, violinist Yehudi Menuhin, 1944. _Right,_ Fritz Kreisler, 1944. ADRIAN SIEGEL. _Below,_ two conductors: newcomer Leonard Bernstein and his mentor Serge Koussevitsky, 1944. BALKIN. _Below right,_ Benjamin Britten, composer of the operas _Peter Grimes_ and _The Rape of Lucretia,_ 1946

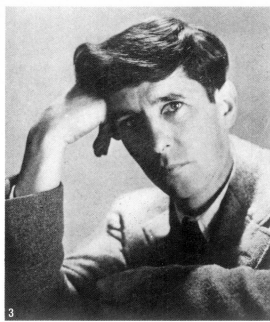

1, Aaron Copland, 'dean of American music', 1947. PENN. 2, Kathleen Ferrier, young contralto star of Britten's *Rape of Lucretia* in 1947. 3, self-taught musician and composer Michael Tippett, 1947. CECIL BEATON. 4, John Cage, 'a highly controversial young composer who has been recognised as a thoroughly talented experimentalist in percussion', 1947. PENN. 5, sketch of The Maestro, 82-year-old Arturo Toscanini, by David Friedenthal, 1949

5

Advertising in Vogue

In America the advertising industry remained fairly healthy during the war, turning over $440 million during 1943. In Britain, however, the face of advertising was changed. During the war years the greatest advertiser was the government. The Ministry of Information published official publicity and propaganda posters, many slogans of which became wartime catchphrases: 'Careless talk costs lives', 'Be like Dad, keep Mum', and Herbert Morrison's pithy injunction to 'Go to It!' There were also informative advertisements to help people cope with rationing and food shortages, showing how to use dried egg, and new ways with corned beef, potatoes, and cabbage.

With production of many goods suspended or curtailed during the war, manufacturers found themselves having to ask their customers to do without their products, or to use them sparingly: 'Unfortunately Cadbury's are only allowed the milk to make a small quantity of chocolate . . . *do* save it for the children.' Many counselled patience: 'Add your name to the waiting list for a new Singer sewing machine' – or as one cosmetics company explained: 'To hasten the return of your service man, our plant is making ammunition fuzes [sic]. So if your favourite store is temporarily out of any Tussy preparation, please be patient.'

Advertisements appeared in *Vogue* for war-related businesses such as the aviation industry or war bonds. If you bought 'E' war bonds subsidised by Textron Lingerie you were entitled to auto-graph a Textron 'Bomb Bond-label' which would be pasted on *'your very own bomb'* to send your greetings to Tojo or Hitler. The wartime theme also crept naturally into advertisements for all sorts of unmartial products. In American *Vogue*, boys in uniform were shown on leave celebrating with a Coke, while a bride and her uniformed groom delightedly fingered their trousseau of Wamsutta sheets. In Britain, the makers of Milton suggested 'Share the shelter but don't share the germs', while Carter's Little Liver Pills were the remedy when 'Wartime living affects your liver'.

More and more, photography was used in advertising. In earlier decades, photographs in advertising were considered bad taste, and drawings were preferred, partly in deliberate contrast with the editorial content of magazines. Many advertisements showed close-up photographs of filmstars who endorsed their products. Merle Oberon, Hedy Lamarr and others lent their names to Maybelline ('the eye-makeup I would never be without': Joan Crawford), while Lana Turner used Max Factor Pancake. Claudette Colbert, Paulette Goddard and Veronica Lake, appearing together in a still from the wartime epic *So Proudly We Hail*, grinned out of the page: 'At Home and Over There it's Chesterfield.' But there were still plenty of drawn advertisements, including Georgia O'Keefe's stunning painting of a haliconia flower for the Dole Pineapple Company, and Salvador Dali's illustration of flying and dancing nymphs for Schiaparelli's 'Shocking Radiance'.

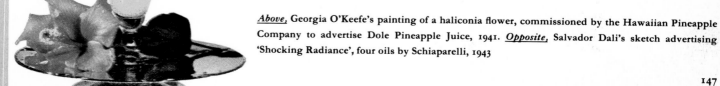

PAINTED IN HAWAII, HOME OF DOLE PINEAPPLE JUICE, BY GEORGIA O'KEEFFE

Above, Georgia O'Keefe's painting of a haliconia flower, commissioned by the Hawaiian Pineapple Company to advertise Dole Pineapple Juice, 1941. _Opposite,_ Salvador Dali's sketch advertising 'Shocking Radiance', four oils by Schiaparelli, 1943

BE A MARINE

The officers and men of the
U. S. Marine Corps ask you
to join them, to wear their
uniform, and by sharing
their common cause to free
a Marine for combat duty.

"Ours is the privilege of fighting for freedom. . . . Never before have the women
of America had such a real opportunity to
serve their country."

Ruth Cheney Streeter

Lt. Col., U. S. Marine Corps

Test Pilot

— SIZE 10

Balanced blending! DuBarry is a

new world
—new woman

WARTIME IMAGES were naturally prevalent in advertising during the war years, both for war-related products and almost anything else. Some advertisements for ordinary domestic goods included an exhortation to join up.

Opposite, advertisement for Wamsutta sheets (when they become available) and joining the Marines, 1944. *Top,* 'Test pilot – size 10: Barbara Jayne's job is to 'first-flight' planes just off the production line of Grumman Aircraft . . . when it comes to caring for her looks, she's devoted to Dubarry Beauty Preparations', 1944. *Above,* advertisement for the Women's Army Corps, 1944. *Right,* 'The man we look *up* to!' Advertisement for Vultee Aircraft Inc., 1942

Above, 'Welcoming a fighting man home from the wars: a happy moment is an occasion for Coke – and the happy American custom, _the pause that refreshes_', 1945. _Opposite above_, 'Hitler came the closest . . . by using the _air_. To hasten victory, our entire aviation industry continues to perform miracles of war-plane production.' Vultee Aircraft Inc., 1943. _Left_, 'Buy Series 'E' War Bonds. This will entitle you to autograph a Textron Bomb-Bond Label which will be pasted on _your very own bomb_. Your greetings will then be sent to Tojo or Hitler . . . While you may not be able to get all the exquisite Textron lingerie, hostess coats, home fashions and menswear you want, there are enough Series 'E' War Bonds for everyone.' 1944

Coke = Coca-Cola

"Coca-Cola" and its abbreviation "Coke" are the registered trademarks which distinguish the product of The Coca-Cola Company.

"I'll Be Right Over!"

MORE DOCTORS SMOKE CAMELS THAN ANY OTHER CIGARETTE!

"Don't mail them, John_ *bring* the Camels_ and <u>hurry</u>!"

Cigarettes, those essential accessories to sophistication and relaxation, were endorsed by the medical profession and film stars, and constituted vital supplies for the armed services. *Above,* 'I'll be right over! – a few winks of sleep . . . a few puffs of a cigarette . . . and he's back at that job again. According to a recent nationwide survey, more doctors smoke Camels than any other cigarette!' 1946. *Left,* 'Home on furlough! –

Bring the Camels – and *hurry*! Camels are the number one cigarette with men in the service', 1944. *Opposite,* Claudette Colbert, Paulette Goddard, and Veronica Lake, photographed on the set of *So Proudly We Hail,* agree: 'At home and over there it's Chesterfield'. Like many wartime advertisements, this one also carried a patriotic message: 'America needs nurses, enlist now'. 1943

152

AMERICA NEEDS NURSES · · · ENLIST NOW

CLAUDETTE COLBERT
PAULETTE GODDARD
VERONICA LAKE

PHOTOGRAPHED ON THE ACTUAL
SET OF PARAMOUNT'S NEW PICTURE

"SO PROUDLY WE HAIL"

AN EPIC OF THE NURSES
ON BATAAN

AT HOME and OVER THERE *It's* CHESTERFIELD

GOOD TOBACCO, Yes . . . the
right combination of the WORLD'S
BEST CIGARETTE TOBACCOS . . .

It isn't enough to buy the best cigarette tobacco,
it's Chesterfield's right combination, or blend, of
these tobaccos that makes them so much milder,
cooler and better-tasting.

Good Tobacco, yes . . . but the Blend — the Right
Combination — that's the thing.

Smoke Chesterfields and find out how really
good a cigarette can be

Chesterfield
CIGARETTES

LIGGETT & MYERS TOBACCO CO.

CARS WERE A CASUALTY OF THE WAR. In Britain, production of cars was stopped for the duration, and there was no petrol for private motoring. America rationed petrol to three gallons a week from 1942. But before and after the war, cars remained symbols of exaggerated luxury and freedom.

Opposite above, 'Jeanette MacDonald chooses plaid for her beautiful Chrysler convertible', 1940. Chrysler advertised 'fluid drive' without gear shifting. *Opposite below,* 'Better expect us *often* – now that we have a La Salle!' 1940. *Above,* 'Humber – at all events, a car you will be proud to own. By appointment to HM the King', 1948

My make-up would not be complete without Maybelline Mascara, Eyebrow Pencil and Eye Shadow. Merle Oberon

NATURAL SUBJECTS FOR VOGUE: advertisements for cosmetics, underwear, and hosiery. Again, they were often endorsed by celebrities. *Above,* Merle Oberon endorses Maybelline eye-makeup, 1944. *Facing page, above left,* 'air-view shades' of hosiery by Vanette, 1940. *Above right,* 'the Esther Williams swimmer's swimsuit' by Cole of California, 1949. *Below left,* the girl in Jergens face powder ('*velvetised* by an exclusive process') holds the medal, 1943. *Below right,* 'Slimmer? But she isn't, darling! She's wearing a Parisienne FLEXEES beneath that travelling costume!' 1940

THE "ESTHER WILLIAMS"

Cole OF CALIFORNIA ORIGINAL

Be his Pin-up Girl!

If you have the ivory-toned brunette coloring of this Pin-up Girl by Varga, the shade for you is JERGENS NEW "RACHEL". To waken the true loveliness of your complexion . . . to glorify your skin-tones and give you the same glamorous look of Varga's brunette "Pin-up" beauties . . .

Varga

Start his head a-whirl
. . . wear the shade meant for YOU in

New Jergens Face Powder

Index

VOGUE

PEACE AND RECONSTRUCTION ISSUE   OCTOBER 1945   PRICE THREE SHILLINGS

ACKNOWLEDGEMENTS

'Bringing out a luxury magazine in a *Blitzkrieg* is rather like dressing for dinner in the jungle!' wrote *Vogue* in 1940. *The Forties in Vogue* is an attempt to reflect the vision, flair, and humour of those editors, journalists, and photographers who not only kept *Vogue* alive throughout all the problems and chaos of the war years – frequently working in shelters or amid bomb debris – but adapted the magazine to mirror this unique period in history. During the war, copies of *Vogue,* optimistic and upbeat as ever, were passed along from hand to hand because of the paper shortage, and played their own small but valuable part in boosting the morale of their readers. British *Vogue's* editor over the decade was Audrey Withers; in America Edna Woolman Chase remained Editor-in-Chief, while the editor was Jessica Daves. Michel de Brunhoff, editor of the French edition, chose to cease publication for the duration of the war rather than collaborate with the Germans. Alexander Liberman, who joined the magazine in 1941, proved a significant and enduring influence; under his art direction the look of *Vogue* changed dramatically. In 1942 *Vogue's* publisher Condé Nast died and was succeeded by Iva Patcévitch.

Once more I am indebted to Alex Kroll, not only for his unerring editorial judgement during the production of this book, but for his firsthand knowledge of *Vogue* and its staff and contributors during the Forties. Other names I must mention are those of Bunny Cantor and Jane Ross for their assistance in *Vogue's* archives, and Jane Cripps for typing part of the manuscript. And of course I am especially grateful to my family, including Debra Walker, who live patiently with the demands of deadlines. *The Forties in Vogue* is for the newest member Adam.